MW01408237

Master The Art Of The Approach

Your Gateway To Luring Any Woman You Desire

By Albert Reese

Introduction

If you're here because you want to understand women better and think that I can help you with that, then you're wrong. No one understands women, and women themselves often say that they barely know why they do half of what they do. Man has done a better job understanding galactic activities millions of light years away than understanding women.

Thankfully, the art of approaching a woman is much, much simpler than all of that, which is why there are men out there (myself included) that are so good at it. As this book will show you, the key to approaching women is not understanding them, it's getting them to understand you.

Table Of Content

If you're browsing this just so that you can skip to the parts you need, then joke's on you, you'll need all of it, ALL of it.

Chapter 1. Reality Check: Deodorant Companies Lie 1

Most of what you know about approaching women is probably wrong, learn the differences between reality and fantasy, as well as the truth behind rejection.

- Myths & Fears: Women
- Myths & Fears: Rejection

Chapter 2. Reality Enhancement: Leveling Up In Real Life 7

Learn how to be confident without being a douche and what you can do to be more attractive without changing who you really are.

- Types of Reality Enhancement:
  a) Overall Improvement
  b) In-the-moment Improvement
- Strategic Grooming: What You Look Like
- Body Language and Behavior: What You Look Like (Part II)
- Dealing With Leveling Up Enlightenment Stress

Chapter 3. The Approach: Location, Lines, & L'Internet........... 39

Some ideas of things you can say to achieve a successful approach as well as where and when they're best said.

- Types of Locations
  a) 'Active' Locations
  b) 'Passive' Locations
  c) Online

- New Possibilities and Whatnot and Whatever

Chapter 4. Conversational Maintenance & Un-approach-ization 99

Never waste a good approach, learn how to make progress, keep her attention, and the proper way to leave while setting up another opportunity to see her again.

- Keeping the Flames Alive: Beginner Mistakes to Avoid vs. Pro Footsteps to Follow
  - Common Mistakes:
  a) Asking Too Many Questions
  b) Filler Words
  c) Being Afraid of Conflict
  - Pro. Footsteps to Follow:
  a) Practicing Answers
  b) Responding Properly
  c) Listening
  d) Fallback Topics
- All Good Things Must Come To An End... Temporarily
  - Getting Contact Details (The Right Way)
  a) Success
  b) Rejection
- ERROR 404: Conclusion Not Found

Chapter 5. Conclusion: The End Is Nigh! 130

Closing remarks and reminders, a.k.a. "My Final Words of Wisdom", a.k.a. "Just Confirming You Actually Understood the Stuff I Said in All the Other Chapters."

Chapter 1. Reality Check: Deodorant Companies Lie

So why put in this chapter at all? Why don't I just give you a bunch of lines that have worked for me and then send you on your way? Because that's an idiotic strategy. Approaching women is not as straightforward as 1 + 1 = 2, there are no "golden lines" that work all the time no matter what, because approaching women is an art and there are different factors and variables involved. I guess you can say it's more like algebra, but unlike those high school tests, this is something you *can* succeed at.

Have you ever seen a deodorant commercial where this guy uses a certain brand of deodorant and it eliminates the necessity to approach because the ladies themselves come running? I know you've seen it, it's the exact same concept for every deodorant commercial ever and though it might seem pretty harmless, it's actually feeding your mind the worst lies you could possibly believe when approaching a woman.

I mean, they always use some buff guy who looks like he's been pulled straight out of the latest chick flick, he's the kind of guy that has no problem approaching and getting approached by women anyway, deodorant or not. Remember, do not believe everything you see on screen. A successful approach has nothing to do with your deodorant, money, or swallowing the heart of a chicken (yes, it *is* an actual Polish superstition), the commercials, movies, and wherever you picked up your fears of approaching women oversimplify and exaggerate things.

So how *did* those girl-magnet guys get like that anyway? Well, contrary to what many rappers claim, they were *not* born with it. There is no mysterious power that the universe gave them and forgot to give to you. Approaching women actually comes with a lot of practice, and of course, you can't practice if you're too scared of everything, so let me highlight some very widespread myths you believe as facts to clear your head of these fears.

Myths & Fears: Women

"No woman would ever want to speak to me, I'm neither rich nor look like Chris Evans."

First off, yes, it true that there are countless gold diggers out there, but it's not fair to the female half of our species to assume that each and every one of them is that way. Besides, you should be grateful you're not rich enough to attract a gold digger, they're nothing but headaches, loud, irritating, Hermès-scarf-wearing, high-heel-clacking headaches.

Second, if we're honest, girls are less shallow and more emphatic than we are (scientifically proven). Of course, being good looking helps, but it's not everything they're looking for. Women are more emotion-oriented and care more about stability than anything else, what's the point of looking like Ryan Gosling if she thinks you're a psychopath? As you go through this book, you'll learn more about becoming more appealing, but for now, remember that a woman is looking for someone who can make her happy, keep her safe, and is someone who she knows will be worth her time (and maybe even her life).

"Women only go for douchebags, never good guys."

No, just, no. Whenever a woman goes for a douchebag, she's not doing it on purpose. She doesn't think to herself, "Oh, look! He's such a pain in the neck, I think I should start dating him!" Whenever a woman goes out with a douchebag, it's because she's confused his douchebag-iness with dominance and strength. What she really wants is someone strong, someone she knows she can depend on. So all you have to do is be that guy, the good guy she can depend on.

"Most women aren't even looking for anything, so why bother speaking to them?"

A surprisingly common misconception, it's understandable why someone would think this, but it's a very stupid thought. While it *is* true that there are times when women want to be left alone, bear in mind that they tend to just stay home and watch TV (or whatever it is girls do) when they don't feel like socializing. Why would a woman be at a bar or party if she wasn't feeling friendly?

Chances are, she's actually waiting, expecting, and longing to be approached. So this is an absolutely ridiculous excuse, and while there will always be exceptions (we can't help it, it's the way of the universe), there is no harm in approaching a woman. Unless you approach her from behind, that is *never* a good idea. It doesn't matter whether you're at a party with lots of people around or if you've already known her a while, you *will* regret it. I have never met a man who hasn't.

Myths & Fears: Rejection

"She's going to say 'no' and then set fire to my hair or get her dog to attack me or [insert another absurd reaction here]..."

This is definitely the most common reason guys ask for help when it comes to approaching women, and it is by far the toughest illusion to get rid of, especially if your only recent contact with a female was your mom. Lots of guys are scared of rejection, especially the extreme kind. For example, they fear that if they say the wrong thing, the girl's going to throw her drink in their faces, or give them a swift kick down there, or do some other extreme thing as shown in movies.

But the truth of it all, even though it might seem a little too good to be true, is that women almost never react that way. Those extreme reactions can only be elicited if you've gotten her extremely mad. Maybe by insulting her family, weight, occupation, cat, anything that she feels strongly about. However, chances are that if you're polite, she'll be polite too even when she tries to end the conversation.

"Rejection doesn't exist."

Propagated by many so-called dating gurus, I appreciate the sentiment, but it's an exaggeration of the truth. The fact of the matter is that rejection *does* exist, your advances aren't going to be accepted by every woman every single time. And what's another way of saying, "Not accepted"? Yep, "Rejected". But don't let this get you down, it's only logical to be rejected. For example, let's say you were holding a piece of a jigsaw puzzle in your hand. Now, what are the chances that by blindly reaching into the box you would pull out a piece that fits the first one?

It's similar with dating, you're not compatible with everyone, but don't let it discourage you, because just as a single puzzle piece is compatible with multiple pieces (one on each side), you are also compatible with more than just one person. There's billions of people out there, and there are certainly going to be quite a few who would enjoy spending time with you. Just be patient and keep trying, you'll find them eventually.

Remember that even when a woman rejects you, you shouldn't let it get to you. She doesn't really know you that well yet, which means that her "no" shouldn't be something you use to measure your self-worth. She's not rejecting you as a person. Seriously, how accurately could she really know and judge you if her only interaction with you was less than a minute long? The rejection is based on her limited knowledge of you, and this projected limited knowledge depends on your approach (the very thing we're going to take care of).

Also bear in mind that rejection can happen for a number of different reasons, it's not always your fault. Some factors are simply beyond your control (what if she really *does* have a boyfriend and it's not just some made up excuse?). So while this book doesn't guarantee that you'll never get rejected again, it *will* help you master the elements that you *can* control to reduce the chances of getting rejected. Soon you'll have so much control over all those elements, you'll be like a real life Aang from *The Last Airbender* (the series, not the movie, *never* the movie).

Chapter 2. Reality Enhancement: Leveling Up In Real Life

Now that I've given you a more realistic view of approaching women, it's time to have a more realistic view of yourself and an old friend called "change". If you've played a lot of video games, then congratulations, today's the day you prove your mom wrong and show her that they actually taught you something. Simple question, what's the biggest difference between a hero when he's just starting out versus when he's at Level 200?

Why do I ask? Well, as it turns out, video games can teach you something very valuable about self-improvement. The core difference between a hero when he's at Level 1 versus by the time he's at something insane like Level 200 or whatever is that the hero himself never changes who he is. He still has the same gloomy origin story and is basically still the same person inside and out, he just has a wider skillset, more experience, and more strength to take on quests.

Now, while I won't go so far as to say that you're a Level 1, the truth is that if you've made it this far into the book, you're most likely not a Level 200 either, which is why we need to start talking about change. *Don't* be that guy that's all, "I only want a girl who'll take me as I am and won't ask me to change," because while that might sound good to you, it's pretty selfish (douche-y) and unrealistic. Remember, a girl is looking for someone she can be happy with and who is worth her time (and I'm pretty sure you're looking for the same), so find a way to *make* yourself worth her time and investment.

When I say "change", I'm not talking about anything stupid and impractical like pretending to like something that you don't, using an alias, or getting plastic surgery (although I think Barney Stinson from *How I Met Your Mother* would say otherwise). The fact that you've come here for help shows that you're still unsure of yourself and your abilities, your self-esteem is too low, and if you don't like yourself, how can you expect that from a woman? (See what I mean?)

One of the essential attitudes to have when approaching a woman is to assume she's going to like you. Remind yourself, "Of course, she'll want to talk to me, why wouldn't she?" You need to have that air of, "I don't have to prove myself to anyone, I know what I am and I'm happy it." That's a sign of stability, strength, dominance, anything and everything she could possibly want in a man. You need to be sure of yourself, otherwise you'll start to get nervous and jittery and she'll be able to sense it, then it's game over.

It's time to become the man, not *a* man, *the* man. *The* man of every girl's dream, *the* man who's not afraid of approaching women, *the* man you've always wanted to be... or, you know, get close enough to it anyway. You're going to have to make some long-term and permanent changes. It'll be difficult at first, but before you start whining, remember that these aren't just for the women you'll be approaching at some point in the future, they're for yourself.

Types of Reality Enhancement: Overall Improvement

These level-ups will affect all aspects of your life, not just approaching women, they will improve your overall quality of life and growth as a person. The first and most important step is to identify what your insecurities are: what is it about yourself that you wish was better? Write it down, list it, go now. I'm not kidding, if this is going to work, you can't be lazy. So put the book down, write, type, video, I don't care, just make sure you produce a list (of your insecurities) we can use as a reference.

Alright, I'm assuming that you're done and that you listened to me. Now, each of the items on your list can fall into one of the following categories:

Physical Insecurities		Mental/Emotional Insecurities	
That can be changed	That cannot be changed	That can be changed	That cannot be changed

Regardless of exactly what the specific items on your list are, *they* are hindering your growth as a person, *they* are hindering you from approaching women, *they* are why you had to buy this book, but fear not! Because although I can't give you a refund, I *can* help you stop them from stopping you from reaching Level 200.

Your first order of business is to become comfortable with and to own up to the physical and mental insecurities you can*not* change. These can include your height (assuming you're done with puberty), certain facial features, mental conditions, physical conditions and more. Worrying isn't going to change anything, so rather than feeling down, the best you can do is accept these insecurities. You don't have to be perfect to get a girl since no girl is perfect. It's part of life that you will have flaws and so will she, so don't stress over the things you can't change.

Now, as for the insecurities you *can* change, the solution is pretty obvious, isn't it? This might sound redundant, but I'll say it anyway, it's time to *change*. Again, you don't have to change drastically and become Mr. Perfect. The goal is to feel comfortable with yourself. You can still be the same video game-loving, movie-analyzing, nacho-munching geek you've always been, but now you'll have to be that *and* someone who is comfortable enough to approach women.

Some examples of adjustable mental/emotional insecurities can include your temper, reasoning ability, maturity, a lack of knowledge, a lack of tact, etc. Basically, intangible qualities that affect the way you feel, think, and interact. Once you've identified characteristics that you feel make you less attractive, make a conscious effort to work on them. There's nothing wrong with admitting you have flaws, it's the only way to improve.

One very common changeable physical insecurity that I think should be highlighted here is weight. As we established at the beginning, contrary to popular belief, women don't have extraordinarily high standards with regards to a man's appearance, *however*, they do want someone who looks like he's taking care of himself. A woman's logic is, "If he doesn't even care enough about himself, could he ever really care for me?"

So although women aren't expecting you to walk up to them with six-pack abs and a weird thing for kale, they do expect to see that you respect yourself enough to invest some time and effort into taking care of yourself. Women love it when a guy is purposive and deliberate in living his life. You need to know (and show) that you're not some lonely loser who has nothing better to do. Instead, you're someone who believes he has things to accomplish and lives in harmony with that belief.

In short, you need to start living your life: make yourself useful, learn new knowledge and skills. It could be anything, from learning a new language to traveling, learning a new instrument to rock climbing. You *don't* have to do something extremely dangerous, elaborate, impressive, or expensive, it doesn't even have to be useful.

For example, I know how to read and write Korean even though I don't speak the language, I know the whole alphabet and can read aloud any paragraph presented to me in Korean, but I won't understand what the paragraph actually means because I don't have much of a Korean vocabulary. I just know what sounds the letters represent, you might think, "Well, what's the point in that?" Well, the point *isn't* to impress anyone. I just learned it for the sake of it, why? Because I take an interest in life.

A meaningful life is made up of all kinds of experiences, whether great or seemingly insignificant. Remember, you don't have to be wealthy to have a rich quality of life. Another great start is getting into a new genre of music, cleaning your room, spending more time with friends and other people (more on why this is absolutely indispensable in the next chapter). Do something that involves conscious and deliberate mental and/or physical participation.

Don't just drift, take control of yourself and your life, shape it however you want. You'll learn more about yourself: your limits, your strengths, and your identity. And once you're familiar with yourself, you can't help but become much more comfortable with yourself, and the ladies will be able to sense that. You don't have to have all your issues sorted out before you begin approaching women, again, it's normal to have flaws, but dealing with them will make you as attractive as possible; you'll be living up to your potential.

These kinds of changes don't happen overnight, they do take time and effort, but they will be worth it. After all, the person who benefits the most from them won't be some girl you met at a bar or on the street, it'll be you. You *will* still be working on these insecurities even after you have no trouble approaching women, so I'm not saying that you have to finish all of them before anything significant can happen. With that said, I believe it's safe for us to now move on to a very different kind of reality enhancement.

Types of Reality Enhancement: In-the-moment Improvement

These changes are all related to your real-time interaction with women. While the last section focused more on very personal changes, this section is more focused on mannerisms and habits present when you interact with other people "in-the-moment". Please note that this section is not to be confused with the content in the next chapter. Chapter 3 is a guide to *what* to say, whereas this section tells you *how* to say it.

You must be wondering, "Well, hang on, shouldn't *what* I need to say come before *how* I should say it?" Put simply, no, because even if I gave you the most effective lines in the history of mankind, they would be absolutely useless if you couldn't even deliver them properly. Even the best tools when put in the hands of an idiot will produce nothing more than rubbish, whereas a single tool (even if it happens to be troublesome) is more than enough for a skilled craftsman to produce a masterpiece. See? Never question my teaching methods, *never*.

I remember this fancy quote by a news reporter in an episode of the CW's *The Flash* that fits into this section nicely, *"It's usually what isn't said that's the real story,"* it's a very versatile quote because "what isn't said" could include things we consciously choose to leave out, our body language, and subtext to what we say, and I know that as you continue reading, you will grow more appreciative of this (seemingly) superficial quote. Let the in-the-moment enhancements begin.

Strategic Grooming: What You Look Like

This is the factor that makes the "loudest" or most obvious impact. You see, getting dressed involves making conscious choices, what you look like says a lot about the kinds of decisions you make. Sadly, I believe that as men, this is where we inherently struggle the most, there's just so many opportunities to make mistakes, and I want to draw attention to the most common mistake of all.

Some of our painfully naïve brothers live by the flawed reasoning that some pieces of clothing work no matter what. For example, they think, "Well, girls seem to like guys in leather jackets, therefore, that's what I have to wear." They go off and buy the leather jacket, but then pay almost no attention when choosing what to wear with it because they believe that the ladies will like them as long as they have the leather jacket, the leather jacket is all that matters.

We can highlight the flaw in this mentality by picturing one of these guys in a leather jacket but with workout shirt and sweatpants paired with it. Cringe? YEAH. This is because it's not the clothes themselves that make girls like you, it's how you wear them that makes the difference. Clothes are a dangerous weapon, you can use them to seriously boost your ratings with the ladies... *but* they're equally as effective in making sure you get as rejected as that *Friday* song by Rebecca Black.

With so much at stake, you obviously can't just copy what some other dude's wearing, find something that works for you; learn how to present yourself in a way that does you justice. "What does that even mean?" you ask? For example, some guys are chubby, and because of this, they can't be careless about what they wear since if they're not careful, they could end up wearing something that emphasizes their chubby parts, i.e. shirts that are too tight and highlight belly bulges, anything with thick horizontal stripes, formfitting jeans, etc.

In those cases, the clothes serve as their nemesis, something working against our chubby bros and driving away the ladies. But it's not just chubby guys who need to be careful, you need to be careful too. You have to make sure that you draw attention to your attractive characteristics and deemphasize the not-so-attractive ones. There's an immeasurable amount of information on what styles are best for different body types, and I suggest you do your research.

Now, this doesn't mean that you will never be able to wear the clothes you like just because they don't complement your body shape. There *are* alternatives, like getting your clothes adjusted at a tailor's or getting them in another color (yes, colors matter too). Your clothes *will* say something about you whether you know it or not, so the goal is to make sure your clothes are saying the right things.

Don't limit yourself, there's nothing wrong with trying something new, and you can have more than one favorite style. So once you've found looks that you like and that you think suit you, run them by some honest friends and relatives. You need their unbiased feedback of whether or not the style looks good on you or nah. Be sure to get more than one opinion and be reasonable when accepting the feedback. Remember, everyone's got their own styles that suit them. It might take some time, but you'll eventually find styles you can rock.

Really quickly, before we move on to the next section, let's talk about personal hygiene (after all, it does technically still fall under "grooming"). Pretty straightforward rules here, just make sure that you're clean and don't look crazy. For the sake of self-respect and the respect of those around you, shower, use deodorant *and* cologne. Would you be attracted to a girl who smelled like week old laundry on a summer's day? Exactly, girls feel the same way too. If they can't even stand next to you, how exactly are things supposed to progress even further?

Important note on facial hair: This is definitely one of the biggest parts of making sure you don't look crazy. Remember, don't grow facial hair simply for the sake of having it. You see, thanks to genetics and other factors, some guys are just physically incapable of growing out a full face of hair. Instead, their facial hair grows unevenly and/or in patches, if you're one of those guys, then you're better off clean-shaven. No facial hair is better than bad facial hair. However, if you do decide to go with facial hair, then keep it neatly trimmed and clean. Longer beards age you, so I definitely advise *against* those, but otherwise, you should be fine.

Body Language and Behavior: What You Look Like (Part II)

Now this... this enhancement: body language and behavior, is more embarrassing and revealing than all those childhood stories about you your mom has ever told her friends behind your back. This is where the largest part of the conversation hinges, and this aspect is trickier than your clothes and grooming because at least you have a general idea of what your clothes are saying about you. However, with body language and your overall behavior (much like those embarrassing mom stories) you're mostly unaware of what they're saying about you and when.

This next part might sound counterintuitive after my saying all of that, but you have to relax. You shouldn't feel pressured after reading everything I said in the previous paragraph because now that you're aware of how important your body language is, you can use it to your advantage. Don't overthink and you'll be fine. You don't need to be a psychologist or a body language expert, It's all about presenting yourself in a way that appeals to women, and the good news is that you need only the basics for that.

Let's go in a somewhat chronological order of the kind of body language and behavior you need to have and when. First up is what you're doing before you even approach the girl. If you're at a bar, party, or some socializing event, always be sure to move around and talk to other people. If you've got your friends with you, relax and have fun with them. This is so that if the girl happens to notice you, she'll note that you're not an antisocial loner who's awkward around people (this also is why we had all those other reformations in the last section).

In her book *Understanding Body Language*, Jane Lyle called stress the "demon of modern society." And no truer words have been spoken. If you start getting worked up, the demon will give you away. If you're uncomfortable, you'll make her uncomfortable too, even on a subconscious level. Show that you're an easy-going guy who people enjoy speaking to, and show that you know how to have a good time. This boosts attraction points because the ladies are mostly looking to laugh and feel good.

Even if you're at a less crowded place or in a setting where it's inappropriate to just start talking to anyone around you, you can still make a good impression by making a conscious effort to improve your posture. Remember, you came here for help because you weren't confident in yourself. This lack of confidence has undoubtedly already infiltrated and poisoned your posture, so you need to search and destroy all traces of this venom.

Here's something you've definitely heard in one variation or another: "Chin up, shoulders back, back straight, stomach in, chest out, eyes looking straight ahead." It's the most common mantra recited whenever someone tries to correct our posture, too bad most of it is WRONG. Yep, you've fallen prey to yet another ubiquitous yet greatly misleading myth (Aren't you glad I'm here to save you?).

The reason the mantra isn't much help in actually correcting anything is because it's addressing the wrong body parts. Your chin going up, shoulders rolling back, back straightening, etc. are only the *results* of what you need to focus on, but they're not what you need to focus on adjusting directly. Don't believe me? Just wait and see. First, go to the nearest long and/or large mirror you can find, stand sideways in front of it, and stay there for all of the following posture adjustments.

Your first target is the angle of your neck, fix this and your chin will automatically go up and your eyes will look straight ahead. Observe the back of your neck, starting from where your neck joins your shoulders going up until you reach the bottom of your hairline, is this part tilted forward? It probably is since this is one of the most common posture problems and is especially common in people who are guarded or "angst-y".

You want your neck to be upright and almost perpendicular to the ceiling. You can achieve this by looking straight ahead while imagining as if someone is using their finger to push your forehead back until your neck is vertical. A common mistake when trying to straighten the neck is pulling the chin back instead of the forehead, the result is an unnatural stance that makes your jawline and neck look shorter. Once you've properly adjusted your neck's angle, you'll notice that your chin and eyes automatically point straight ahead, wasn't that easy?

Now it's time to fix your upper back and shoulders. A common mistake is simply throwing your shoulders back. Sadly, this is not guaranteed to fix your posture because the normal tendency of throwing your shoulders back is that your neck moves forward and you look like a chicken. Instead, focus on the center of your chest, specifically the top of your sternum (a.k.a. the dip where your collarbones meet) and imagine it was an open box filled to the brim with coins, and that you need to keep the box upright so that the coins don't fall out.

Focus on raising just your chest (sort of puffing it out) and trying to keep the "box" (your sternum) upright. You'll notice that your shoulders immediately go back without even trying, and your neck, instead of tilting forward, tends towards an upright position. The results of fixing your posture this way look way more natural and make you seem taller.

The last of the major upper body adjustments is your core. Similar to the previous adjustments, the angle of your lower back from your pelvis should be somewhat vertical instead of tilted forward (which would make you sort of look like a shrimp). One way to correct this properly is to think of those senior citizens with walking sticks, have ever noticed how bent they are from the stomach up? Well, that's essentially what you look like if you don't take care of your core. I mean, at least the senior citizens have an excuse, and (assuming you're not yet already a senior citizen and/or aren't suffering from some relevant medical condition) you don't.

Now for your lower body, starting with the pelvis. Surprisingly common in men, the biggest problem here would be an anterior pelvic tilt, which is amusingly and eerily appropriately also referred to as the "Donald Duck Syndrome". This is when your pelvis is tilted forward, making your buttocks and stomach stick out more than they're supposed to. And while this looks attractive on (and is deliberately done by) many females, as a male, this isn't exactly how you'd want to walk up to a woman.

Now, it's normal for a pelvis to be slightly tilted forward, but if it's tilted forward too much, it'll negatively affect your posture for your entire upper body. This next part is going to be more difficult if you're one of our meatier brothers because we'll be using two bones. Specifically, your Anterior Superior Iliac Spine

(ASIS) and your Posterior Superior Iliac Spine (PSIS) and the angle they make as the reference to check if you have the Donald Duck Syndrome and then fix it if you do.

You don't have to, but I recommend taking your shirt off for the self-assessment. To identify your ASIS, which is on the front of your pelvis, stand sideways in front of the mirror and put your hands on your hips (the side of your abdomen), automatically your hands will be on top of your hipbones. Now trace your hipbone with one of your fingers until you come to a relatively sharp bony ridge on the front of your hip, this is your ASIS. Mark it with something to make it more visible, a marker, Post-It note, whatever.

Next, you have to find your PSIS, which is on the back of your pelvis. This is slightly harder to find because it's less prominent, but there's less muscle on top of it, so you should be fine. Place your finger on one of the dimples at the bottom of your spine. Then move your finger an inch or so away from the dimples and to the outer side of your back (if you're using your right hand's finger placed on your right dimple, then move about an inch to the right, if you're using your left finger, move towards the left). The PSIS will also feel like a bony protrusion or lump, mark it once you find it.

With both your ASIS and PSIS marked, try looking at the angle they make. Note that it is normal for the ASIS to be around 7° lower than the PSIS, and that it is abnormal if your ASIS and PSIS are level. However, if you can see that the PSIS is significantly higher than your ASIS (more than 7° higher), then I regret to say that you, my friend, are a Donald Duck, but fear not! There *is* a way to fix it.

Okay, just to get the bad news out of the way first, unlike all the other adjustments I've had you make so far, there is no single exercise you can do to correct Anterior Pelvic Tilt (APT) right away. Instead, you're going to have to do a full-on routine, and I can't give you a personalized routine because I have no idea what other back and/or bone conditions you might have. But the good news is that APT is relatively simple to fix and there are many free routines online. Of course, if you have any conditions, you must consult with a doctor first because this is not something to be taken lightly.

However, I can give you some general stretches for you to try out, just be careful when doing them, take things slow, and don't push yourself too hard. First, the Quad/TFL stretch ("TFL" as in "Tensor Fasciae Latae", ugh, that has got to be the most stuck up name of a muscle ever). Staying as upright as possible, and maybe even holding on to a wall with your left hand for balance, bend your right knee, lifting your right leg up just enough for you to wrap your right hand around your ankle. If you don't feel a stretch, gradually and gently tug on your ankle until you feel a light burn, hold for 30 seconds if you can and then switch sides.

WARNING: DO NOT, I REPEAT, **DO NOT** ATTEMPT THE NEXT EXERCISE IF YOU HAVE LOWER BACK PROBLEMS. I will not take any responsibility for any damage you inflict on yourself. I mean,

I run away from my own responsibilities all the time, I don't have time to take on any of yours. Your stupidity is your own responsibility. Be careful, man.

Find a chair and sit on the edge of its seat. The chair should be high enough for your thighs to be almost parallel to the floor when you're seated. Next, move your knees apart while keeping your feet planted flat on the ground, make sure you have enough space between your knees for what's about to happen next. Then, bend your whole upper body forward until you can place your hands flat on the ground and hold it for 20 seconds. Then sit back up again, and repeat.

Know your limits, if you're a bit on the chubby side or if it's been a while since your last workout, then it's normal if you can't get your palms completely flat on the ground. Don't force it too much, or else you could end up tearing something, listen to your body. If it's screaming, "STOP! STOP! I'M DYING!" then listen to it. You only have one body, take care of it. Obviously there are tons of other effective APT-fixing stretches out there, and you should definitely get professional help, but I don't have time to deal with here, so I'm leaving that up to you to take care of.

And finally, I know this is going to sound weird, but we're going to improve the posture in your knees. This adjustment is slightly less related to how you look, but more on the benefits for your later years. While standing in front of your mirror, start contracting your quads. This actually takes off some of the pressure on your knees and reduces your chances of suffering arthritis later on in life, you can do this repeatedly at any time throughout the day.

Observe yourself in the mirror once you've made the adjustments and notice the improvement in your appearance. Of course, you'll still have to get used to all of them. One of the reasons it's so hard to make these postural changes is because the muscles in these areas are usually dormant (or inactive). So try to be more conscious of your posture and keep practicing. Eventually proper posture will become second nature to you, and as Lyle says, "Change the body, change the mind. Change the mind, change the body." So not only will you look better, you'll feel better too.

Okay, so we've tackled the things you should work on before approaching her/ Now here are things to keep in mind during the actual approach. Again, I'll be telling you *what* you can say in the next chapter, this section is all about *how* to say it. Naturally, you can always come back here once you're done with the next chapter.

First up is how far away you stand from her. There's a whole branch of nonverbal communication called "*Proxemics*" which is dedicated to determining the effects someone's proximity has on your behavior and vice-versa. You've probably already told someone (it was probably one of your parents) at some point of time to respect your personal space, either physically or metaphorically, but did you know that Proxemics has even *measured* what technically counts as "personal space"?

Technically, your personal space extends to up to a 4 foot (1.22 m) radius, with your "intimate zone" comprising the first 6 inches to 18 inches (16.24 cm to 45.72 cm). The people who study Proxemics (Proxemicists? Proxemists? Proxemicismists?) have observed that when someone steps into another person's intimate zone, both persons' heart rates increase and their blood moves to their extremities. It has also been noted that these reactions are preparation to either run away or do other things that will require muscle use (including intimate acts).

Since the invasion of someone else's intimate zone can be seen as either threatening or romantic, make sure you do *not* enter this zone unless you're sure the other person is comfortable with you. At the beginning of the conversation, stand 2-3 feet (0.61 m – 0.91 m) away from her. Once you're sure she's comfortable, gradually inch closer at certain points. Standing too far away gives the impression that you're only interested in her as a friend, whereas moving closer creates chemistry and is a silent reminder that you're interested in a romantic way.

Depending on where you are and on her background, it should be fine to have reasonable physical contact even during the first encounter. By "reasonable" I mean shaking/holding hands, standing next to each other such that your arms are touching, and if she's really comfortable, even putting your arm around her waist or shoulder. However, don't overdo it, especially since this is the first time you're seeing each other; you can't be creepy or needy.

Her private parts are off limits, especially during the first few hours of meeting her, and depending on the circumstances, even for much longer after that. Make your romantic interests clear, but don't look desperate. Just so you know, girls enjoy playing the game too. If you let yourself get "caught" too easily, then there's no fun left for them anymore and they'll quickly lose interest in you.

Remember, if you're comfortable with yourself, you won't be begging her to stay. Even if the conversation gets interrupted temporarily, you need to stay calm. You can even use it as an opportunity to move around and talk to other people some more, and this will once again remind her (and yourself) that you're not a loner and that you're a "chill" person.

What if while you're moving around and talking to people you notice that another guy has gone up to her and started flirting? Don't panic. If you start getting worked up, she's going to see you as possessive and insecure, and we can't blame her 'cause that's what it is, an insecure person's reaction. Would the alpha lion be worried if a weaker lion tried to rival him? Of course not, because the alpha is sure of himself and knows that he can take his rival down.

By keeping your cool, you'll impress her with your reasonableness. However, make sure that you reaffirm your interests. You don't want her to think that the reason you're unaffected is because you're no longer interested in her. Balance it out by not panicking when another guy is talking to her but by also making the effort to reconnect with her when possible, perhaps after she's finished talking with the other guy. It's a delicate balance, but if you succeed, the chances are that you'll be looking more appealing than any of the other guys who try to hit on her.

Also, if there are pauses in your conversation where neither of you are speaking, don't let them bother you. It's natural to have pauses since no normal conversation is non-stop all the time. If you start to get nervous about the pauses, it'll give the impression that you're someone who's easy to fluster or agitate, and this will make you seem weaker and unstable in the girl's eyes.

Now, let's talk about how you use your voice. When you're nervous, your heart beats faster and your breathing speed increases as well, this gives you a more breathy and higher pitched speaking voice than normal. Calm yourself down beforehand and remind yourself that men have been approaching women for thousands of years. Take deep breaths before approaching her and remember that this is just another normal part of life. It's sort of like driving a car: it can be intimidating and you'll need some assistance at first, but you'll eventually get better with practice, and eventually you'll be doing it effortlessly.

By calming yourself down, you'll be able to speak normally and without rushing your words. Further, speaking in a deliberate manner reinforces the image of you being someone with purpose (remember what we talked about before?). Let's be reasonable, you don't have to sound like Morgan Freeman (and you shouldn't try to), but you *can* sound natural, confident, deliberate, and masculine.

And I'll only be addressing this one relatively briefly, but let's talk about hand gestures. Now a large part of this is cultural and there's nothing wrong with using them. However, if you're one of those people who doesn't use them that often, then make sure you know where to put your hands, otherwise you'll draw attention to them and look really awkward.

In addition, you need to remember to smile (properly). Everyone looks better when they're smiling correctly (otherwise they just look creepy). Remember to avoid grinning because it gives a goofy and immature impression, making you look almost like a kid. And don't smile unless it's appropriate, smiling is a great start to being friendly, but no normal person is smiling every. single. second.

Instead, you can try "peppering" the conversation with occasional smiles to express approval, commendation, and even to relieve tension. Most dating gurus recommend a somewhat lopsided smile with either minimal or no teeth showing. Don't try to laugh without showing any teeth though, because not only would that be creepy, but it would be *so hilarious* for everyone around you. Remember, you want to look like you're enjoying her company, but don't look *so* overjoyed to the point where it seems as if you're someone people don't usually speak to.

Of course, your mouth's smile isn't the only thing on your face. Your mouth, eyes, and well, basically the sum of all the parts of your face make up something commonly known as a "facial expression". There are countless ongoing debates between psychologists about the origins of specific expressions such as smiling or the furling of eyebrows, but one thing is for sure, your facial expression matters, *a lot*. The face is the part of our body that's stared at the most during a normal conversation. It's like a giant billboard on the side of a skyscraper: you can't hide it.

Did you know that even people who are born blind and have never seen another person's reaction in their lives also smile when they're happy? They've never seen a smile before or have even been told how to do it, but they still do it. And according to some very smart scientists, it's likely because many of our facial expressions have been genetically ingrained in us. With this in mind, you need to start being more careful of your own expressions. Have you noticed any habitual expressions on your parents or other relatives that you find weird? Well, don't judge too harshly because you may also unknowingly be making the same expressions too.

Here I'm going to highlight something that you probably haven't thought of before, and that's where the real danger lies. I mean, you obviously already know that you have to laugh when someone says something funny, you know how and when to display surprise. And at times, you can even fake anger or fake sadness when you feel like you're supposed to care about something but don't actually feel anything. All of those expressions are part of things we learned through our experiences and interactions with other people.

However, your most dangerous adversary is the one you're not conscious of: your neutral facial expression. Also probably known to some of the younger readers as one's "resting face". Basically, it's the face you make when you're not making a face. This is your face's default setting. The expression that you have when you're walking around aimlessly with nothing particular on your mind, or when you're casually flipping through the pages of a magazine, or when you're not reacting to anything or trying to express anything. Yes, *that* face.

To find your resting face, you're going to need a mirror again. Relax all your facial muscles, and then face the mirror, pretend you're bored while waiting for a bus. No, it's not that the bus is late and you're in hurry, just imagine that you got to the bus stop a few minutes early and instead of going through your phone, you're looking straight ahead at nothing in particular. You can even use a chair for this exercise if you think it'll help you. The face you see in the mirror will be your resting face (more or less, because goodness knows if you managed to do the exercise correctly).

This is probably the first time in your life you've paid this much attention to your neutral expression, you might have even been surprised by it. Sad to say, regardless of your reaction to your resting face, not everyone's neutral face sends out a neutral message. For example, lots of people unwittingly look angry all the time, just look at Kanye West, Anna Kendrick, and the Queen of England... Yeah, probably best if your resting face didn't look like any of theirs.

Sure, you need to look masculine and strong, but you shouldn't look intimidating or pissed off because then no one's going to want to speak to you, and the whole point of this book is to help you speak and get spoken to. You might be one of those rare cases where your resting face involves your mouth hanging open and (unless you have a medical condition that needs you to have it open) you need to keep your mouth closed because it's honestly sort of off-putting to look at.

If you're one of those people whose resting face looks as ticked off as Kanye's, then try softening it. Believe it or not, there have been serious and legitimate scientific studies into what it is that makes certain resting faces "express" contempt. In fact, some women are even getting plastic surgery to "fix" their intense/angry resting faces. Of course, like I said before, I'm not going to ask you to resort to something as extreme and expensive as plastic surgery. No, we're going to take care of this organically.

First off, it's not as hard as it sounds. You technically only need to worry about your resting face when you're interacting with other people, meaning that you only really need to be conscious about your resting face during conversations. Second, the results from all those studies on intimidating resting faces show that it's mostly the subtle facial cues that make the biggest differences.

During a conversation, you "wear" your resting face while you're listening to another person talk. You can soften your expression by flashing a very slight smile, it barely even can be described as a "Smile". It's more like a slight tilt of the ends of your lips upwards, aim to do it so subtly it's barely noticeable. Also note the use of your eyebrows. This sounds like a long shot, but some people furrow their brows while listening even when they're not angry and you might be one of them without realizing it. If you are in fact one of those people, then make a conscious effort to avoid repeating it, especially around strangers.

It's definitely important to pay attention to all parts of your facial expression, but the most intense part of it is your eyes. Now, psychologists say that eyes which are fully open yet relaxed are perceived as the most pleasant and friendly. However, I do *not* recommend that you try to apply this because there's too much room for error. You might end up widening your eyes too much and then look like you're in a state of perpetual surprise or as if you're constantly trying to pick a fight (HA!).

Instead, if you've been told you have an icy and/or intimidating pair of eyes, then we're going to soften them with the final aspect of your body language and behavior we'll be considering in this section: eye contact. I recommend you practice maintaining solid eye contact beforehand with friends and relatives because this is one of those things you're not going to be able to just "wing". According to those cliché Instagram posts, our "Eyes are the window to the soul," or was it Shakespeare who said it first?

Regardless of the origin, the saying *does* have some truth to it. Our eyes convey more emotion than we would like them to. So looking her in the eye is going to be challenging, especially if you're not already used to making eye contact during conversations. Your goal is to maintain stable and comfortable eye contact while speaking to her, and *please* try to accomplish this without being creepy.

The ability to maintain eye contact shows her that you're able to "hold your own", so to speak, and that she doesn't intimidate you. Also, eye contact provides you with valuable information on how the girl you're speaking to is feeling. You can use it to more or less accurately gauge your progress and how comfortable she is with you. Speaking about comfortableness, remember that it *is* possible (and very common) to intimidate someone with just your eyes.

A few paragraphs ago, we were talking about softening your expression, but instead of trying too hard to change the shape of your eyes, we want to reduce the intensity of your eye contact to a comfortable level. Yes, look her in the eyes during the conversation and while listening to her, but consciously offset the eye contact with subtle actions like looking at the ground or somewhere else while laughing. And if during the conversation you need to think or recall something look up or to your side instead of straight at her.

For example, imagine she asked you for the name of that actor in that movie, the one with the things and the blablabla. If it just so happens that you feel you've been making too much eye contact and want to lower the intensity so you don't scare her off, (even if you remember the actor's name) you can look away from her and maybe look towards your left or right and go, "Ugh! What was his name? Hang on, uh..."

Some people close their eyes when they're trying to remember something, you can do that too. Basically, eye contact is important, but if you feel as if it's making her uncomfortable, then look for subtle ways to break it off every now and then. All of this especially goes out to the dudes who have naturally intimidating stares, but the principles still apply to everyone since too much of anything is bad. But of course, you'll be fine as long as you never underestimate the power of the eyes.

Dealing With Leveling Up Enlightenment Stress

I'm sure that after going through this chapter, you've realized you've got a *lot* of things to work on, but don't be discouraged. No one expects you to have all these changes down within a week, they all happen gradually with time and practice. The important thing is that you're now aware of them and can work towards them. The best (and probably the *only*) way to achieve all these level ups is by avoiding doing too much at once.

Be smart and set reasonable and progressive goals, start out with things that are just outside your comfort zone, because if you go too big too early, you'll find yourself paralyzed and completely unable to accomplish anything. As you reach your smaller goals, you'll be better equipped to set and accomplish slightly larger ones. Work on a maximum of 2-3 things at a time. In fact, this is the perfect time for another cheesy quote, "If something's worth doing, it's worth doing well." and naturally, it's impossible to do anything well when you're trying to do 5 things at once.

You shouldn't be irrationally scared that you'll never be able to approach a woman until you've perfected all of the level-ups because approaching women successfully comes with practice. I simply highlighted all those level-ups to give your practice some direction and improve its overall results. The truth is, you'll probably already be successfully approaching women before you're even halfway through with your self-enhancement. Keeping this in mind, it's about time we finally moved on to the things you can say as part of your approach.

You've learned quite a bit up until this point, so before we move on to the next chapter, let's synthesize what we know so far so that we'll be better able to see how it all fits into the next chapter.

Chapter 1 addressed your fears and misconceptions, I sincerely hope that you genuinely have a more realistic view of women and the art of approach because if not, then that means all the stuff that I said after that as well as the stuff I will say after this point will be absolutely useless. You're not going to succeed 100% of the time, but you're not going to fail 100% of the time either.

Approaching a woman is like showing her a preview of who you are, and of course, previews are limited so make sure you're highlighting your virtues or "good side". Even if she doesn't want to continue the conversation, remember that she's deciding based on your approach ("preview"). She's not rejecting *you* as a whole, however, you can reduce your chances of getting rejected if you learn how to present yourself right.

Chapter 2 has been focused on enhancements, "level-ups" that not only lead to a more stable, satisfying view of life and yourself, but also to higher attraction points. Being comfortable with yourself contributes to being comfortable with other people. We also had a thorough discussion of how to *not ruin* a woman's impression of you, but the truth is that we've barely even started. All the level-ups are mostly applicable to starting a conversation, but we haven't even begun to talk about what's involved in keeping the conversation going, we'll deal with that process in Chapter 4, so let's not get ahead of ourselves.

Yes, my apprentice, I've shown you (a small part of) the technique (the "*how*"), the next chapter is where I hand you the tools you'll be using (*"what" to say*) to create a masterpiece of an approach.

Chapter 3. The Approach: Location, Lines, & L'Internet

Well, we've gotten to the part that most of you probably thought would've been Chapter 1. These lines or "templates" of approaches are going to be divided and arranged by the contexts they can be used in. Each section is a stand-alone, meaning that it's not directly connected to any of the others, therefore, this is the *only* chapter of the book where I'll approve of skipping pages.

There are three main categories of locations and you're welcome to start off reading any category you feel is most relevant to your situation or you would personally find easiest. However, bear in mind that each kind of location provides you with different experiences and insights, so it's better if you read and try out all three categories. The three categories are:

Active Locations	**Passive Locations**	**Online**
Locations where you're expected to socialize and no one will find it weird if you start walking up to and talking to	Locations where spontaneous flirting doesn't normally happen, it would be considered strange to simply start	Pretty self-explanatory, this is when you approach women online before meeting up in real life.

complete strangers. Examples: bars, parties, meet-ups, etc.	talking to just anyone. Examples: class, shops, restaurants, etc.	Examples: Facebook, Tinder, etc.

Under each category of locations, you'll find the following:

a) ***List of General Rules for that Location***: These apply to each template in the section.
b) ***Settings***: Basically, "sub-locations" of each category (Example: Active -> Bar/Club, Passive -> Grocery Store, or Online -> Facebook).
c) ***Templates/Lines***: Openers that can be adapted and changed as needed.
d) ***Advantages/Disadvantages***: I put these in here in order to highlight the specific reasons a specific line works and what you need to look out for when you use it. In fact, if you pay enough attention to these points, you may eventually be able to craft your own template/line to use.

Do your best to be honest no matter which location and approaches you choose. You don't have to lie to a woman to get her to like you, just be positive and keep things light, it'll make her feel comfortable and glad that you two started talking. Also remember that location doesn't matter, approach does; In other words, you'll be able to get a girl no matter where you are as long as your approach is on point.

NOTE: Most of these approaches are "templates" rather than specific one-liners. This means that you can adapt them to situations. For example, instead of just a long list of specific questions you can ask her during your approach, I'll be teaching you *what kind* of questions to ask so you can formulate your own to suit the situation. Of course, I'll also give you some examples too as samples for you to look at and get an idea of what you're aiming for.

Finally, all of the following approaches are non-exclusive to their settings, I've simply grouped them under the settings I personally think they work best, so you're free to change to use any of the following approaches wherever you deem appropriate. However, with that said, it's best if you didn't switch an active location opener with a passive location one or vice-versa. You can switch out an active location opener with another active location opener if you feel that the situation calls for it, but there's a reason I separated the active location lines from the passive ones, alright?

Active Locations

On the surface, these situations seem like the most intimidating: There's lots of people around, usually some very loud music, and she's got her friends with her, but in reality, this is one of the easier locations because the girls in this situation are expecting to be approached, so you can be pretty straightforward here.

I. General Rules:

1. Her private parts are off limits. I said this before, and I have just said it again. If you go for any physical contact too early, she'll get uncomfortable. And if you go for her private parts too early, you'll get rejected. No matter where or how you meet her, be respectful of her.

2. Always use a friendly and casual tone, some of these lines can be taken the wrong way if said with the wrong tone. In fact, you might even end up offending someone if you're not careful. Always smile and consciously monitor the tone of your voice during approach.

3. Always introduce yourself as soon as possible after saying the line/template. I won't always tell you, "...and then introduce yourself" because it's common sense. The earlier you introduce yourself, the better.

4. Make a habit of repeating her name back to her. You may end up chatting with several girls, and it would be a terrible first impression to forget their names within the first few minutes. Once she tells you her name, you should use it in the conversation as soon as possible, this is a basic memorization technique. For example, "Well, Annie, now that you mention it..." "Thank you, Rosa." "Can I ask you something, Steph?"

5. Avoid words such as, *disturb (as in, "Sorry to disturb you…"), interrupt, bother, etc.* because they subconsciously give your approach a bad connotation. Also, you don't have to apologize for being sociable, only apologize for mistakes or inconveniences, if ever.

6. Again, you don't want to look lonely so it's better if you go out to these places with at least two other friends. Obviously, you guys don't have to stay together the whole time, but having them with you will at least allow you to say things like, "I'm here with my friends" or "You would not believe what my friends and I saw/did earlier tonight…" etc.

7. Don't get too drunk. As a beginner, you want to be in as much control over what comes out of your mouth as possible. It's okay to drink and have a good time, but if your main goal of the night is to practice approaching women, then alcohol will be working against you.

II. Lines and Templates To Use:

- Direct Approach:

"Hi, my name is ________, I thought I'd be sociable and come over and say "Hi". What's your name?"

Advantages	Disadvantages
This can be used at **any** of the active locations. It gets right into it and immediately gives her information about you, making you more "accessible" to her and subconsciously letting her know that you've let down some of your guard and you're encouraging her to do the same.	It's pretty short, so its success more or less hinges on *how* you say it and what you look like, so make sure you say it in a way that exhumes confidence.

A. At a Bar/Club

- **About Her Drink**

"That looks interesting, what are you having? [Wait for her response]. Oh, is it good?" or if you've already tried the same drink before, say, "Oh yeah, I've tried it before, I found it..." then describe it, was it strong? Interesting? Funny-tasting?

Advantages	Disadvantages
Works with any girl with any drink.	This immediately introduces the whole opinion vs. opinion, if you're too serious, it'll look like you're trying to be preachy

	and impose your opinion onto her.

You could also try guessing what she's drinking, "Ah, is that a ______?" If you're right, you can introduce yourself and go on talking about the drink, when you last ordered it, where you think they make the best version of it, etc. If you're wrong, then you can joke about it and say something like, "Yeah, this is why I got kicked out of bartending school." And continue from there.

Advantages	Disadvantages
Works with any girl with any drink.	Once again, your very first line is very short, if you don't say it right, it'll get very awkward very quickly, which is especially difficult for a beginner to deal with.

If her glass is empty, you could say, "Hey, I can get you another drink if you'd like. I'm planning on getting a _____ for myself..." If she accepts, buy drinks for both of you and continue the conversation. If she doesn't want another drink, then order a drink for yourself and introduce yourself, maybe talk about how often you come to that particular bar or who you're here with.

Advantages	Disadvantages
This method immediately makes her feel positive about you since you're being so generous.	Depending on what bar you're at, her drink might end up being *expensive*, I do *not* recommend doing this with more than two girls in one night.

- **About Your Drink**

Sit at the bar with your drink until someone you like comes to order. If you're already familiar with the drink she ordered, smile at her and say, "Interesting choice, I've had that before..." then compare it to the drink you're having at that moment, is her drink stronger? Does it taste better?

Then ask her if she's ever had whatever you're drinking before and depending on how the conversation goes, you could recommend it to her or joke, "You like it too? We should start a fan-club!" Don't worry if she doesn't like the drink though, we'll have a detailed discussion on dealing with conflict in Chapter 4.

Advantages	Disadvantages
This approach is very subtle and looks as if the conversation happened almost completely by accident.	You could end up waiting a while, so don't make this your primary method, instead, use it as a secondary one for when you've moved around enough.

- **Dancing**

If she's just finished dancing and has sat down to rest, do not approach her right away. Give her a few minutes to cool off and catch her breath because you don't want to catch her when she's tired and not up for a conversation. Once you think she has rested enough, approach her and say, "You had some great moves on the dance floor earlier, but thanks to you I wasn't able to dance to that song I liked 'cause I knew you'd make me look bad."

Advantages	Disadvantages
A compliment which lets her know that you're paying more attention to her relative to other girls. Optional add-on: "...knew you'd make me look bad. How are you going to compensate for making me miss my favorite song?" (Reminder: be honest. If it wasn't your favorite song that was playing, then say something like, "...miss such a great song?"	Be extra vigilant with how you use the tone of your voice for this one. You can only use it once you've actually seen her dance. Just imagine how awkward it would be if you said the line and she's like, "But I just got here, I haven't even danced yet." That would be pretty sad, man. Pretty sad.

A similar approach is going up to her and saying, "I was planning on dancing with you, but then I changed my mind because I realized you'd just make me look bad."

Advantages	Disadvantages
By saying, "...planning on dancing with you" instead of saying, "...asking you if you wanted to dance with me," You again exhume confidence because the subtext is that you're assuming that she would like to dance with you. By watching out with these subtle word choices you can drastically change her perception of you.	The same as the previous approach.

B. At a Party:

As I mentioned earlier, you can still use the **direct approach** at the beginning of this section since it works in any active location. The direct approach is basically just letting her know you're being sociable at a social event... you can't go wrong there. Here are some openers adapted specifically to parties.

- **If She's Alone**

Focus on how you know the host, "[Host's name] did such a great job with this party, right? [Wait for her response] I'm _____, a friend of [Host's name]'s by the way. How do you know [Host's name]?" Of course, you'll have to adapt the last part to your situation, if you're a colleague of the host, or even a friend of a friend of the host, then say that instead.

Advantages	Disadvantages
It's a pretty natural opener, and a bonus is you seem like you're enjoying the party instead of being antisocial.	The very first line could potentially evoke a simple yes/no answer since it's not an open-ended question. If she only gives a one word answer, you're going to have to respond quickly and introduce yourself right away in order to stop things from getting awkward.

If you don't know the host that well and only know his/her name, you can say (in a lighthearted tone), "I'm going to tell you a secret, I don't really know who [Host's name] is, I'm just here for the food and drinks." Or even, "I'm just here to dance." Of course, even if she knows it's a joke and laughs along, it would help if you clarified very soon after the opener that you actually do know the host and that you're not just some weirdo off the street who thought it would be a good idea to crash a party.

Advantages	Disadvantages
This is a great example of keeping things lighthearted and fun. Of course, you want to impress her as a responsible, driven person, but this line immediately shows her that you know how and when to enjoy yourself.	In very rare cases (but especially if you don't say it in the right tone) she's going to take you seriously and her very first impression of you will be that you're a creep/jerk, and remember that first impressions last (scientifically proven, but more on that in Chapter 4), so you'll have to put in extra effort to disprove it.

You could also approach her and say, "You seem like a girl who likes to..." then make a positive guess as to what she would like to do. For example, "You seem like a girl who likes the beach," or "...likes to sing," or "...likes to travel," then respond appropriately when she asks you why you think so.

Advantages	Disadvantages
You can evoke a smile almost immediately with this opener.	You need to have a legitimate reason for the adjective you used, for example, for "likes the beach" you could say, "because you've got a great tan". You're going to have to

	observe her for a little bit before you can start.

- **If She's with Friends**

Your main goal should always be to engage the entire group, at least initially. Remember, you're technically an intruder/outsider to their group, so if you just step in and start talking to one of the girls, the others might feel as if you're "killing their vibe". And if there are guys around, they'd naturally be protective of their female friends and might view you as a "threat".

A great setup is to walk around with some of the party's snacks (you can either swipe the entire bowl or let the host know ahead of time that you're volunteering to pass around some of the snacks). Just grab a bag of chips or whatever snacks they're serving at the party, and offer it to people around you. Eventually, you can casually make your way over to her group of friends and say, "Anyone for more nachos/chips?"

If some or all of them say that they would like some, as you give them more food you can ask their opinions about the food by simply saying, "They're great, aren't they?" or turn to one of the friends who declined and say, "You don't want any? Why not?" Then you can say something like, "Well, personally, I rate the nachos/chips a [insert positive rating] and the dip a [insert positive rating], what do you guys think?" and then introduce yourselves and carry on from there.

Advantages	Disadvantages
Another smooth and natural opener. You're almost always immediately perceived positively since you're bringing something good: food.	This will take some extra time and effort, maybe even some planning beforehand.

Another way to engage the group would be to ask them for some facts or information while using your friends as context. For example, after telling your own friends what you're about to do, you can walk up to her group of friends and say, "Hi guys, my friends and I are trying to figure out..." then pick a topic that's not political or sensitive and ask for their help with it.

For example, "Hi guys, I'm here hoping you can help, my friends and I are trying to figure out whether Australia also observes Daylight Savings or not, do you guys happen to know?" If the girl and her friends ask you why you're asking them instead of Googling the answer you can make an excuse along the lines of, "Well, we'd like to see how many people agree with my answer versus how many people agree with my friends' answer before we find out the truth."

Just in case you were wondering, the answer to the above example question is that some parts of Australia observe DST while others don't, in the end, no matter who the girl and her friends side with, everyone's right. I recommend that you choose questions similar to the one above: questions that most people haven't really thought about, questions that people wouldn't be too embarrassed or scared of getting wrong.

Similarly, you can also ask the group for their opinion on something instead of a fact. For example, "Hi, I'm just dropping by really quickly as part of a survey my friends and I have bet on. Which is the better theatre snack, popcorn or M&Ms?" You might even call your one or more of your other friends over to help keep the conversation going even further. You can adapt the opener to ask their opinion on anything as long as you stay away from sensitive topics.

Advantages	Disadvantages
It's a great way to subconsciously tell any males in the group that you're not trying to look better than them and that you respect them enough to even go to them for "help".	If you pick the wrong topic, then you're just going to end up hated by the group; some safe topics are food, clothes, gadgets, the location of the party, etc. Some unsafe topics are politics, religion, morals, ethnicities, I'm not saying that you have to act as if you don't

	care about those topics, I'm just saying that a party (especially a party where there's booze around) is not the right place to be discussing such sensitive and serious topics.

If it just so happens that everyone in their group of friends is female, you could try this more lighthearted approach, "Uh-oh. You girls look risky. I can tell just by those looks in your eyes you've got some evil schemes planned for tonight, don't you?"

Advantages	Disadvantages
When said write, you make the group laugh almost instantly. You're almost immediately on everybody's good side. The line's absurdity turns it from a potential insult into a playful joke coming from a guy with a sense of humor.	When saying the line, don't stress the word "evil" too much because they might take it the wrong way. It might sound like you're telling them they look like the kind of girls to do "evil" or immoral things and in effect, calling them "easy". Yikes.

- **Formal Parties**

Well, sorry to disappoint you, but I'm not going to give you any lines or advice here because I'm a firm believer in "no dating at work" policies, there's just too much at stake and things can get super complicated if you date someone from your company or workplace. So don't expect any help from me with this.

C. *At a Wedding*

At first, I wasn't sure whether to put this down as an Active or Passive location, but I went with Active because it's more or less expected that people connect at weddings and start dating. Of course, you want to be respectful of the newly wed couple's big day, especially if you're close to them. One way to do this is to starting hitting on people only at the reception (the part after the vows have been said and everyone's just eating, drinking, and making bad speeches).

If you were being observant, by the time reception rolls around you would've already spotted a few girls you're interested in. The reception seats are usually assigned at weddings, but that doesn't mean it's hopeless. You have a chance whenever people are allowed out of their seats, like to grab food from the buffet or to dance.

- **About the Food**

Once you have the chance to approach her, you can say, "It's great that [Bride's name] and [Groom's name] finally got married, huh? Thanks to that, we were able to have all that delicious food." If you say it with the right tone, she'll laugh, then you can clarify that you were kidding and even throw in how you know the bride and/or groom in your introduction and then carry on from there.

Advantages	Disadvantages
Humorous, it puts your approach in a positive light.	Only works after you've had food (duh).

- **About Her Appearance**

This is one of the most obvious ones, girls spend more time than men in preparing for weddings. I know, they always spend more time than men when it comes to getting ready in general, but weddings are days when they expend extra effort and acknowledging this effort is definitely plus points in their books. For the best results, use a specific compliment.

For example, "Hi, I know we've never met before, but I just had to let you know that your dress' shade of blue really suits you." Or even, "Hi, I know we've never met before, but I just had to say that that is a beautiful opal necklace you've got on, and an even more beautiful smile to go with it." Adapt your compliment to anything she's got on, her accessories, dress, hairstyle, etc.

Advantages	Disadvantages
This is a quick way to make her blush and fluster her (in a	If you overdo it, she might think you're gay. I'm not using

positive way) since such a direct and respectful compliment from a stranger is sort of unexpected.	that as a derogatory term, I just mean that it's common knowledge that gay men are usually more stylish, and for the purposes of this book, you don't want her to think you're gay because your romantic interest wouldn't be clear to her. Therefore, your compliment should just be specific, but not sound like you're an expert on this stuff.

Another great line you can say about her appearance is, "I can't believe no one's mistaken you for the bride yet, you look stunning."

Advantages	Disadvantages
This is great because you catch her off guard with a pleasant surprise.	I can't really think of any disadvantages except for, well, imagine how awkward it would be if you accidentally said it to the groom's ex-girlfriend. Although, what are the chances that the groom's ex would be at his wedding? So...

D. At Speed Dating Events and Singles Mixers

These events are where you can throw all subtlety out the window because everyone at these events is single and is actively looking to change that. This means you can hit on her/ask her out very directly and even reference your conversations with other girls freely. Note that the introduction is the very thing that happens in most of the following openers because these are places where the sole purpose is to actively market yourself for a date.

- **Asking Her Opinion**

For example, "Hi, I'm _____, and you are? [Wait for response] Well, it's nice to meet you <u>[Her name]</u>. Just a quick question, if I were to let you pick a spot for our date, where would you take me? You see, other girls have promised me a restaurant or a movie, which are great, but I think you seem a lot more interesting than that. So, what would you pick, and why?"

Advantages	Disadvantages
This shows her you're confident and sociable enough to be talk to other people because you're not a loser who's making her the only chance he has at getting a girlfriend.	There's a chance that she may take this the wrong way because again, the line assumes that she'd like to go on a date with you anyway.

It's a perfect way to get her to start imagining the two of you together.	So try to smile warmly to let her know it's not a serious question, you're just trying to get to know her.

You can also try, "Hi, my name is ____. What's your name? [Wait for response] Well, that's a very nice name, [Her name]. So, what do you think about the event so far? I mean, I think it's great, but I think you seem like you would've organized it a more interesting way if you had the chance."

Advantages	Disadvantages
It's part-compliment, part-small talk. Even if this was your first time ever in approaching a woman, the line instantly makes you look like an experienced socialite. I mean, it's SMALL TALK for crying out loud.	This isn't exactly the most memorable of lines. It's pretty useful in getting her to think and it can show you a bit of what she's like, but you'd better find have an interesting question/topic right after this one in order to really spark her interest.

- **Acknowledging Her Appearance**

Again, this is one of those events where everybody puts a little more effort into the way they look. You should try to acknowledge that effort but then focus on more important things. For example, "Hi, I'm ____. You are? [Wait for response] It's nice to meet you, [Her name]. Your blouse looks great, by the way [Allow for response, if any]. It's really suits you, I saw you from across the room earlier and told myself, 'Man, I HAVE to speak to the girl in the pink blouse.'"

From there, she'll probably smile or laugh and say something along the lines of "Well, I'm here now." or "What did you want to say?" or "What now?" To which you can say basically anything. You can make small talk, use another opener, or ask her a question. Just make sure you don't go back to discussing her appearance again, you have better things to talk about.

Advantages	Disadvantages
This allows you to set the topic and direction of the conversation to basically anything.	When picking an aspect of her appearance, stay away from talking about *any* of her body parts (even so called "romantic" references, such as the eyes) because it comes off as creepy, especially since this template involves you saying, "I saw you from across the room."

III. Conclusion: Active Locations

These are the best practice grounds for someone who isn't used to making new friends often, and I recommend that you focus on these more at least initially because these environments will help you hone your social skills. They basically allow you to talk to anyone you want for as long as you want (or as much as they can take). Remember, you do not have to apologize for your presence because you are not a negative impact on their vibe, you *own* the vibe.

Get to know as many people as you can (and not just so that you can look popular, but that's a bonus too) and connect with them. However, being at these locations does not guarantee success, not everyone will like you and vice-versa, but only real losers let that get them down. Although, these environments can be a little hard on the ole wallet, so be smart with how you work.

Passive Locations

These are areas where spontaneous socializing could, but doesn't necessarily, happen. Here, it would be sort of weird if you walked up to a stranger and started talking all of a sudden. Obviously, you'll be taking a very different approach to active locations. With these, you'll need to find some excuse or other to start talking to a girl you like, which is why I don't recommend starting with these locations if you're not already used to talking to strangers.

Of course, there's nothing new about using passive locations as "hunting grounds" to meet women. In fact, here are some common lines that men have been using for decades, "Excuse me, Miss. Do you have the time?" or "Excuse me, Miss. How do I get to [some place or store]?" Iconic, classic lines that have served men well since long before any of us were born.

The problem is, they can't serve us anymore. Imagine walking up to a woman and asking her for the time when we have both watches *and* smartphones as staples in this modern world. You can also find out where anything and everything is thanks to all the different navigation apps and location-enabled hipster food picture uploads. Thus, man has been forced to come up with new lines and templates. Read on, dear apprentice, and gain wisdom.

I. General Rules:

Rules 1-4 at the beginning of the Active Locations section apply here too.

5. Don't do anything that would make you look suspicious. Don't cover any parts of your face (even if it's with a scarf in the middle of winter) and approach her with your hands visible, i.e. not behind your back or in your pockets.

6. Be extra careful with your word choice. Remember that from her standpoint, you're a complete stranger who has no reason to be talking to her, so she's most likely already a little

uneasy, your words should get rid of this uneasiness, not make it worse.

7. Be extra careful with how you spend your time at these places. People and cameras will be watching at all times, and you might unnecessarily worry them and attract suspicion by loitering in the area with no clear intentions. Spend a maximum of an hour at these locations. It's okay if you leave an area without finding anyone to talk to, you can always come back some other time or move to another location.

II. Lines and Templates to Use:

- **Direct Approach** *(we also talk about this under Location C.)*

This approach can be used in basically any of the passive locations, just make sure you pick the right time, "Hi, I'm ______. I know that this is bizarre since we've only just met, but I just wanted to let you know that I think you're pretty [or insert another compliment]." If she responds happily or thanks you, you can follow up with something like, "If you have to go somewhere right now Is it okay if we exchange numbers [or add each other on Facebook] so that we can have a proper chat when you're free?"

Advantages	Disadvantages
This identifies you and your intentions immediately. It clears away the suspicion of you being a criminal or whatever. By saying, "I know this is bizarre…" you show that you're social-smart and aware that this isn't a conventional way of interacting,	It's definitely very strong given the setting and it's relatively difficult to transition into a regular conversation after being so forward, but hey, it gets the job done.

A. *In a Shop*

Personally, I think these are the best passive locations because you have some control over what kind of people you're going to be meeting. For example, if you're an avid reader, you can go to a bookstore and meet fellow book addicts, you can even "refine" your search of people by going to sections of the store containing genres and titles you like and meet someone with tastes similar to yours. And of course, this principle applies to almost all every kind of store.

- **If She's a Customer**

Do NOT attempt this if you're working at the store, not only will it get you fired, but it makes you look sad and desperate. Also, most of the templates here probably wouldn't make any sense if they were used by someone who actually works at the store. For example, "Excuse me, miss? Hi, I don't mean to be a bother, but I was hoping if you could tell me which of these I should try first?"

Advantages	Disadvantages
Obviously, this works best if you're actually holding two products when you ask her the question. Again, with "I don't mean to be a bother…" you show that you know that people don't usually talk to strangers under these circumstances while also transitioning into why you're talking to her.	Unless she leaves the store first, you're probably going to end up buying the product she chooses because if she happens to see you leave without buying anything it'd be obvious that the products were just a ploy to talk to her.

If you see her looking at merchandise or something that you like as well, you could say, "Hi there, I just saw you looking at that and I just had to ask, are you a fan of <u>[insert brand or whatever she's holding]</u> too? 'Cause I happen to be a huge fan."

Advantages	Disadvantages

Provided she's not in a rush, it's a pretty great way to transition into a long and personal conversation almost immediately and effortlessly regardless of her answer to your original question. It's very subtle and makes it look like the conversation happened almost by pure coincidence, so you'll definitely look less creepy with this approach.	You might notice that this approach and the last one don't introduce you right away, and yet I've emphasized (repeatedly) that the sooner you introduce yourself, the better. The reason for this is because in passive locations especially, the thoughts going through her head once you approach her is, "I don't know this guy, what could he want?" She's on guard, so our first priority is to letting her know why we're speaking to her. Once she's less uneasy, the introductions can follow.

Don't worry, you still have a shot even if you see her holding a product or merchandise of something that you're not familiar with. For example, let's say she's looking at an album of a band that you've never heard of before, you could say, "I was looking at that earlier too, but I wasn't sure whether to buy it or not, is [the band's name] good?" this works even if you're at a grocery store and she's holding some snacks or drinks.

Advantages	Disadvantages
Same as the previous approach.	Same as the previous approach.

Another line is, "Excuse me, Miss. Sorry to bother, but could you please give me a quick suggestion for a gift? I need to get my [cousin/niece] something and I'm terrible at picking gifts for [teenagers/kids], she's [age] years old and [a phrase or two describing her; for example: 'is very outdoorsy' or 'likes animals']." This is most effective when you're at a clothes store or even a bookstore.

Advantages	Disadvantages
The reason this is so frequently used and can even be called a "classic" is because it actually does work.	Its advantage is also its disadvantage. Since it's so well known, the girl might figure out what you're trying to do and this could spook her or make her less receptive even if you look like a decent guy.

- **If She's a Salesperson/Cashier**

In my opinion, this has got to be the best situation a passive location could offer because unlike if she were the customer, you'll always know where to find her since she works at the shop. However, it's important to always remind yourself that the shop is her place of work, show some respect for her and her job by not saying or doing anything that could get her fired. For example, if you're interested in speaking to the cashier, then make sure there's no line behind you before you try.

Now, the shop personnel will either be friendly (mostly because it's their job) or annoyed (mostly because of the customers at their job), here's how to deal with both of those moods. For example, let's say you're shopping or browsing and a cute salesperson comes up to you. If no salesperson approaches you, then you can just pick up one of their products and walk up to her with a question about it just to get the conversation going.

Depending on what kind of shop it is and the product you're holding, you could ask a question along the lines of, "Do you have this in another color?" or "Do you guys sell any other [books/albums/works] by this person?" or "Do you have any recommendations for what goes well with this?". Just be sure to not ask questions that you could have answered yourself. For example, asking, "Is this product part of the sale?" when there are large print signs designating which sections of the store have products on sale and which do not.

After she has answered your question or helped you with something, you could say, "Wow, they have nice customer service here, if you speak any longer, you would probably find a way to convince me to buy everything," an optional line you could then add is, "You're doing a great job, but I'll have to be careful with how I spend my money when you're around. [While holding wallet] See? My wallet feels lighter already."

Advantages	Disadvantages
This isn't something she hears every day her and it's definitely going to put her in a good mood. It's playful yet not disrespectful to her place of work.	You'll probably end up buying something, which is why don't pick up anything too expensive or something you don't need. In fact, it would best if you just do this on top of your ordinary shopping, killing two birds with one stone, so to speak.

However, if she doesn't seem very friendly or is in a bad mood, smile at her first. I guess you could ask her what's wrong, but since you're a stranger to her she probably won't talk about it with you. The simplest way is to ask her for a recommendation, "Excuse me, Miss. I hope I'm not disturbing you, but I'd like to try one of your bestsellers. What would you recommend?"

After she shows you the product, while smiling at her you could say, "Okay, but only because I trust you." Only at some point after that do I recommend you asking her if she's okay because you'll already have some sort of friendly connection no matter how small it might be.

Advantages	Disadvantages
Again, you show off your social awareness skills by being polite, it shows her that you know something is wrong, but you're not here to aggravate her, you just have something to say. Not to mention, you automatically get plus points in incentive for her to talk to you since you're asking her something as a customer.	Being in a bad mood, she could reject you instantly, you could be in the middle of saying, "Excuse me, Miss-" when she says something like, "Sorry, sir. Not now, I'm busy," just as an excuse to stop talking.

If you're feeling extra generous, you could even get her something small from the store as a way of telling her to cheer up. For example, cashiers at convenience stores are usually in a bad mood, while she scans your items into the system, you could casually grab gum/candy/chocolate from two different brands and say, "If you had to pick, which one would you say is better?" Then buy whatever it is she picks and give it to her.

She'll be all, "What? No way, sir. This isn't necessary, etc." If she's saying it while smiling you could joke saying, "Please keep it. I had an ulterior motive anyway, I wanted to see you smile." However, if she's still not smiling after you give her the thing, you could say, "Please keep it. It's a small way of thanking you for your hard work." She can't argue with that, it's a well-meaning gift from a well-meaning customer, it will make her feel good and she might be extra nice to you the next time around.

Advantages	Disadvantages
This is definitely the smoothest thing you could do in this situation. Not to mention, if you guys end up dating eventually, think of what an epic memory of a first time conversation this would make, she'd be proudly telling all her friends about how sweet you were and whatnot.	Since you're at the cashier, there's probably a line behind you. If not, great, you can have a short conversation and get her contact information. If there's a line, then I'm afraid you only have time to do this opener, but at least you can always come back when the shop is less busy and try talking to her again.

Of course, you can still talk to her without getting her something small (in some stores it's even impossible to get her something either because they don't sell anything small or whatever they're selling is still unreasonably expensive). If it's one of those small shops where the cashier is the only staff around instead of having other people as salesladies, then you can use the earlier templates for salesladies since that's probably part of the jurisdiction of her job.

Another way would be to talk about why you're buying certain items while paying, and then ask her if she relates. For example, if it's a furniture store, you could say, "I get almost all my DIY stuff from here. [Store's name] makes/sells some really great products [or "has a nice selection"]. Right now, I'm working on [some project or part of the house]. Do you also like DIY projects?"

Advantages	Disadvantages
You could adapt this to cashiers of any kind of store: clothes, games, books, furniture, even stationery. Another seamless transition into learning something personal about her and having a friendly conversation	Again, there might be other customers behind you also waiting to pay for their stuff, so you'll probably end up exchanging only a few lines.

Just to finish up this section, I'll just remind you again that I'm giving you these lines as something you can do while shopping. I am *not* saying that this should be your primary way to meet girls since it could get pretty expensive really quickly if this was your primary method if you know what I'm saying.

This is preparation just in case while shopping you see a girl you'd like to talk to approach. If she's a customer, then you obviously have to get her contact details by the end of the conversation, but if she's a shop employee, then you can obviously go a bit slower (and sometimes you might even *have* to thanks to circumstances).

B. At a Restaurant

I'm not a fan of trying anything at restaurants because approaching another customer is practically impossible. Think about it, no one likes being disturbed during a meal, the maximum time s/he would give you is a few seconds of bothered attention. And do I even need to remind you of how scary girls are when they're starving and waiting for their food to arrive? Dude, they're the walking dry land versions of piranhas.

If a cute girl happens to sit at the table next to you, then *maybe* you could use some of the lines from the previous section by asking her for a recommendation, something like "Excuse me, Miss. Sorry to bother you, but I was just wondering if you could suggest something for me to try? I always order the same thing whenever I come here and I was thinking of mixing it up a little [tonight/today]. What do you think?"

Advantages	**Disadvantages**
There's that display of social awareness yet again.	You can only use this if you haven't ordered anything yet.

Problem is, how often do cute customers just happen to be sitting all alone at a table next to you? If there's a cute girl but she's across the room, what are you going to do? Shout, "What would you recommend?!" just so that she would hear you? Ugh, I'm cringing just thinking about. Don't waste your time looking for girls in these locations. However, if you spot a girl you like while you're in a restaurant, you could wait until she gets up to leave and then take your chances in our next location...

C. On the Street

The most effective method here would be to use the direct approach, because really, do you have a choice? At the very beginning of the Passive Locations section, we discussed two iconic lines that were mostly used to speak to women on the streets. I also showed you why they are problematic considering our technology-saturated world. However, if you really want to, you can try making the second icon work, "Excuse me, Miss. How do I get to <u>[some place or store]</u>?"

Advantages	**Disadvantages**
It gets the job done, it grabs her attention and gives you a chance at a conversation.	She's expecting you to end the conversation quickly. After all, why would you be asking for directions if you don't need to be there? As a result, she's

	more likely to feel annoyed if you keep talking to her.

- **Direct Approach**

Here's a reminder of what the **direct approach** says, "Hi, I'm ______. I know that this is bizarre since we've only just met, but I just wanted to let you know that I think you're pretty [or insert another compliment]." Some examples of other compliments that work are "...you have a great smile." Or "...you're very stylish." Although it's true that compliments about her personality would be more meaningful, under these circumstances, you really don't have anything to go on except for her physical appearance.

The main reason I say this is the only practical method on the streets (and the best method in all passive locations) is because instead of looking for an excuse to talk to her, you're telling her frankly why you want to speak to her. You're also making it clear that you're not there to harm her or be a drag in anyway, you're simply showing an interest in her. Another advantage of this approach in the long run is that it might even keep you out of the friend zone.

South Koreans have an expression which roughly translates to, "treating her as a woman", basically, the gist of its meaning is that you treat her as a potential partner rather than simply treating her as a friend. This approach does that, you show your interest and treat her "as a woman" because your words show that you're paying attention to her femininity. If your approach is successful and as you get to know each other better, the dynamic of your relationship would be as two people who may or may not date instead of just two friends.

D. In University/Course/Class

Ah yes, just like high school all over again. This is another great hunting ground because you have higher chances of running into the same girl again. You'd be surprised at how many celebrities actually married people they met in university. Depending on how big the campus is, you and the girl will be on some very different orbits, so to speak. Let's start with the closest you can get to a girl at this point...

- **She's Sitting Next to You**

...or right behind you or right in front of you, whatever. This is the best of the best case scenarios in a university setting. If it's your first time meeting her, then you can open with, "Hi, I'm ______. And you are? [Wait for response]. Nice to meet you, [Her name]. Hmm, on second thought, I think I'm having mixed feelings about sitting next to you. You seem like you'd have no trouble passing this class and I'd look so bad in front of the professors." Or, "If I sit next to you and you constantly raising your hand and you know all the answers, you're gonna make me look bad."

Advantages	Disadvantages
This is great to use the very first time you meet her since first impressions last. From the time you use it, she's going to see you as a positive and fun dude.	It's a bit of a long approach and a sort of rollercoaster. You're telling her something positive, "negative", then positive again. Remember, if this is your first time meeting, she's pretty anxious too.
This makes heavy use of banter, and I like to think that "banter" is just the baby sister of "flirting", but more on that in Chapter 4.	Which is why you need to make sure that you move on from the "negative" bit as quickly as possible.

- **She's In Your Class**

One of the biggest differences between university classes and high school classes is that professors don't usually leave much space for free time (Of course, that depends on the university itself, but I'm speaking in general here). If the time table says 2 hours, then the professor uses up the whole 2 hours, maybe even more. Because of this, you don't make your move until after everyone's out of their seats and on the way to their next classes.

Chances are that you guys have already spoken even a little bit, but if for some reason you guys haven't, then you can try something like, "Hi there, I'm ____, just really quickly before we leave, I have a complaint. You can't just smile suddenly in the middle of class because I can't help but stare and I always lose track of what the professor's saying. It's almost like you're trying to make me fail on purpose. Admit it, you are, aren't you?"

Advantages	Disadvantages
Actually, now that I think about it, you can even modify this line to work on somebody you've already spoken to. The "I have a complaint" is a great way to instantly grab her attention. Once you mention the compliment, it gives her a sense of relief even if the suspense was synthetic.	If you're known as a serious person who rarely jokes around, or you give off that sort of aura, then you need to be careful. I would normally recommend saying the "I have a complaint" part with a straight face and breaking out into a smile when saying the rest of the line. However, we don't want to give her a heart attack. So if you're normally perceived as quite serious, then you should say the whole thing while smiling.

- **She's In Your Friend's Class**

Coordination is really the best thing strategy in this case, but if you want to talk to her without getting anyone else involved, then here's what you can do. Once your class is done, you can walk straight to where your friend's class is under the guise of waiting for him. If your friend comes out first then keep him talking right next to the classroom door until the girl you're interested in comes out of the class.

If you're directly facing the door while talking to your friend, she's most likely to at least glance your way or notice you (after all, how often do people just stand right outside the door and talk?), when she does, flash her a smile. You can pause your conversation with your friend automatically by saying, "[Still smiling], Hi. Whoa, hang on. You're in this class too? [Allow for response, if any]. What's it like being in the same class as [Your friend's name]? You should be glad you're not in my class though, I think my snoring wouldn't let you hear anything the Prof says."

Advantages	Disadvantages
This definitely makes you look like some awesome social butterfly. From her perspective, you're chilling with your friend and still have enough sociability to shoot a compliment her way. Looking good, my man.	A lot of this depends on opportunity, she may or may not notice you, and there goes all your hurried walking just to be there on time. Or your friend may or may not show up to class that day, and there goes your excuse to be there. See? This is why I recommend

	coordination between you and your friend.

If you decide to cooperate with your friend/s in order to get closer to the girl, then I congratulate you on making a wise decision. You could get your friends to throw a party and invite both you and the girl you like, you could even ask them to introduce you to her, or find out some of her interests. Yes, there are basically no down sides to having a collaboration.

If your friends throw a party just to give you a shot at her, then you can use the lines from the Active Locations section of this chapter. If they find a way to introduce you, then you don't even need to have an approach because they took care of it for you, just skip to Chapter 4 of this book for tips on how to keep the conversation interesting and productive.

- **If She's On Your Campus**

...but neither you nor your friends have any direct contact with her, then the best time to approach her is during break time or whenever it is you run into her, be it before or after the school day starts/ends. If she's eating alone, you could approach her, smile, and say something like, "Hi, I'm ____, can I join you? I promise to not take any of your food when you aren't looking..."

Advantages	Disadvantages

It makes her laugh and makes it look like you're seeing her for the first time regardless of actually how long you've had a crush on her. It's a very flexible line because you can say it in almost any tone with almost any facial expression and it will still sound goofy due to its unexpectedness so early in the conversation. It sort of implies that you're speaking out of guilt of stealing other people's food, the thought of which girls find funny.	I can't really think of anything you might want to look out for, surprisingly enough. Note that even when the whole line is said with a super serious face, as long as you break into laughter right after it, you're still good to go.

- **Bonus: She Asks For A Favor**

Maybe you're one of those guys who studies well or has something that would be useful in one of your classes, if so, you might actually be approached by a cute girl who needs your help. However, just because she approached you first doesn't mean that you can be careless. As a potential provider of help, you already sort of have the upper hand, the things you say should ensure that this doesn't change.

Let's say you're minding your own business when a cute girl from your class/year approaches you asking if you had notes from that lesson in that class both of you share, she says her name and smiles while waiting for your response, you could say, "Hi _____, it's nice to meet you. Yes, I do have the notes but I'm only sharing them with you because you're so cute [or another positive thing like, "...being so nice about it." Or, "...because you have this charm I can't explain."]."

Advantages	Disadvantages
The flirt immediately makes it clear that she can't chuck you in that dreaded friend zone just yet. First impressions last, this is one of the smoothest first impressions you could ever make.	You're welcome to paraphrase all of the templates here, of course, but beware that when you paraphrase this particular template you don't make it sound like you're extorting her or something.

III. Conclusion: Passive Locations

If you read the Active Locations section before the Passive Locations, then you must have already noticed that our approaches for passive areas are slightly more polite or formal than those for active locations. This is because our first priority in a passive location is to always reassure the girl we're approaching that we mean her no harm. After all, approaching a complete stranger just out of the blue is relatively unconventional in these places.

Unlike in active locations, in passive locations you always need to justify why you're approaching the girl. Here it is even more imperative that you smile, I won't accept any responsibility if you end up in jail just because you looked suspicious while approaching someone. Again, you are responsible for your own stupidity, I've already done my part to warn you of certain consequences.

Online

Over the years, this has become more and more common. In fairness, it is somewhat cheaper and is more convenient than going out to meet people in real life, and it has shown some success, I actually know a guy who ended up marrying someone he met online. However, this is my least favorite category for beginners to practice both verbal and non-verbal communication.

For example, how are you supposed to improve your eye contact skills? Or how do you hone your social skills or your ability to improvise? Texting and online communication give you lots of time to think out a response, however, real world interactions don't work that way. The real world requires you to be more spontaneous and to respond quicker. Yes, it's trickier, but it's the most natural way to improve your interactions with women.

So if you decided to read this section first with the intentions of making this your primary method of approaching women, then I suggest you snap out of it. Yes, snap out of your crazed delusion. Seriously, man? After I gave you all that awesome advice in Chapter 2, *this* is how you "apply" it? I agree that online dating is a fast and cheap way to meet people, but you need to practice meeting people in real life first. I mean, unless of course you plan on all your relationships being perpetually and purely digital until the day you die. Anyway, let's begin.

I. General Rules

1. Never get serious with a girl unless the two of you have video called each other, you never know who you're talking to on the internet. Man, I am dead serious about this, it is the first and most important rule of online dating.

   We always see ridiculous news stories covering what people call "catfishing" and think that it could never happen to us. However, those are the stories of the stupid catfishers that got caught, the really skilled ones are so good they don't end up on the news. BE CAREFUL.

2. When complimenting a girl, it's best to not focus too much on her physical appearance. Beautiful girls have already heard that they're pretty in every way possible. If you want to stand out, then take advantage of the fact that you have

access to their profile, talk to her about common interests and her posts.

3. Many people are more disrespectful on the internet because there's this illusion of no accountability. However, remember that the internet gives the whole world access to what you say or do. If words in real life can never be taken back, then words on the internet can never be killed. Think before hitting the "Submit" or "Send" button.

4. Keep your profile up-to-date and full of positive things about you. Treat it like a CV for online dating, this is what potential partners will look at to decide whether to keep you or not. Ellen DeGeneres is great at finding stuff like this. She goes through the profiles of people who will be attending her show, then shows their most embarrassing pictures and posts on national TV.

   Her logic (which I agree with 100%) is, "If you're fine with putting it on the *Worldwide Web*, then why would you get upset if I showed it on just one country's TV network?" Anything that you wouldn't want a girl you're interested in (or Ellen DeGeneres) to see must be deleted.

   I'm not telling you to post every single detail of your life online, not only is that annoying to other people but it's actually also dangerous for your sake. In fact, you might even dislike people who post that frequently, but if you're going to use the internet as a way to reach girls, you should at least present yourself properly on it. You need to show her *why* she should bother chatting with you.

It would be best to also take down pictures where it looks like you're lonely or not having fun. For example, maybe there's a group picture where everyone's smiling and having fun while you're standing awkwardly and seem separate from all the fun they're having. An instant way to jumpstart your social life and get some good photos out of it is by joining meet-up groups. Make sure to get comfortable when taking pictures and try to genuinely enjoy yourself.

5. Do not come on too strong. Don't like or comment on every single picture or post she has, in real life, that would be equivalent to following her around and telling her how awesome she is even for just breathing. Play it cool. We've already discussed the importance of not being clingy in Chapter 2 and that still applies here.

6. I'm not against the use of emoticons, but I suggest you use them with caution. Except for maybe the smiley emoticon, I see no reason for you to use an emoticon when you're messaging her for the first time. Of course, emoticons do serve some great purposes, using one or two during a flirt could enhance your game, and you could even use emoticons to drop hints, but using too many gives you an immature (maybe even feminine) appearance.

II. Lines and Templates to Use:

Unlike all the Active and Passive Locations, there is no "best" template that I think can be applied in all online locations. Online dating is complicated in its own way. For example, with Active and Passive Locations, the only thing you have to go on before you start talking to a girl is her physical appearance, which is why you can use roughly the same template on any girl as long as the kind of location is the same. However, with online dating, you are given a chance to learn about a girl before you even speak to her, always use this to your advantage, it will increase your chances of getting noticed.

A. Facebook And Other Similar Social Media Platforms

This is the easiest way to meet someone on the internet, especially if you want to do it for free. In fact, I like to think of these platforms as the online versions of passive locations. Much like in a university or school, there's different levels of closeness you can be with a girl even if it's just online. Let's see the closest starting point...

- **You've Already Met Her in Real Life Before**

Most likely she is a friend of a friend, or she's someone in your year, or in your department at work. Regardless, if you manage to have a conversation or two in real life, make sure that you add her and message her within a week of that conversation. Once she accepts your friend requests, comment and/or like one or two of her new posts.

The comment doesn't have to be long or over-the-top, it can even be as simple as, "Great picture! Wish I was there." Or "Interesting, I never thought of it that way." This makes her feel positive and gives you a better chance of her responding in the next step, a direct message. Since you'd just met her in real life recently, you could say something like:

"Hi [Her name]. It's me, _____, from the [where you last saw her] the other [day/night]. I'm glad to see that you're doing well, I just wanted to say that I enjoyed our chat and was hoping we could continue it here since you seem like a fun person. By the way, I noticed you [something from her profile. For example: "have a cat"], [Question about what you noticed. For example: "What's its name?"]"

Advantages	**Disadvantages**
I'd say the set-up is 60% of the success, if done right, it will make your message look casual and relaxed.	Beware of digging too deep into her profile. If you aren't careful, you might end up referencing a post that's over a year old, and that would give off a *very* strong "creepy stalker" vibe.

- **She's a Friend of a Friend**

You should always strive to find common ground to talk about, in this case that would be the friend you share. Obviously, the first thing you would do is send her a friend request. If you have taken good care of your profile like I told you to, then getting your request accepted won't be a problem. Once she accepts, go through her profile. Be sure to take your time, if you message her too soon after she accepts the request, then it would look pretty lame.

Once it's been at least a couple of hours since she accepted the request, you can carry out the whole exercise from the previous approach of commenting on a couple of her posts. After commenting, switch to a private message and say,
"Hey _____. Noticed you were also friends with [Your Friend's Name], I just saw [him/her] the other day and we had fun chatting over a couple of drinks [or insert some other positive thing about how you know your friend or what you did with him/her recently]. Anyway, just thought I'd message you and let you know that I think you're cute."

Advantages	Disadvantages
With the setup, not only does this look natural, but the part about your mutual friend makes you look like some suave social butterfly.	The sad thing is that this is still the internet. If in the real world she has no obligation to talk to you, it's even truer online due to the lack of

	accountability only the virtual world can provide.

- **You're Total Strangers**

This is when you added her out of the blue. As in, she was in your suggested friends and you have no idea why, but you added her anyway. Once she accepts, comment on a couple of posts and check out some of her interests. If you manage to fine one or two common interests, you could say, "No way, you're a fan of [whatever it is you both like] too? I've been a huge fan of [whatever it is] ever since I [...explain how you got into it]. What about you? How did you discover it?"

Advantages	Disadvantages
You're immediately starting off with a positive connection. You're giving her a deeper reason to reply to your message.	This approach depends on the chance that you both like something, whether it's a hobby, show, person. What if you seemingly have nothing in common?

If you can't find anything on her profile you can relate to, then talk about yourself. Be brief, to the point, and positive. Remember, your goal is to show her why she should bother talking to a complete stranger on the internet. Tell her about your interests, maybe even your age, and other cool things about your life in an interesting and humorous way. It's probably best if you keep it to six sentences and below.

For example, "Hi there! Just here to introduce myself real quick and also say a small thank you for accepting the request. I'm Jason, a 28-year-old architect with a fear of heights (oh, the irony). I should also warn you that I live and breathe everything related to the Game of Thrones, swimming, and animals (I hope to one day be the architect who owns a dog). Now that you know a bit about me, can I learn a little about you? Because so far, all I know is that you're cute and seem interesting. :)"

Advantages	Disadvantages
Casual, showcases your friendliness. It ends with a compliment and invitation to reply. This makes it easier for her to actually reply because you've already given her an idea about what to say. This is great on social media sites like Facebook where the platform's main focus is *not* dating. As you'll see, we take a very different approach on an actual dating website.	It's actually more difficult than it may seem at first because we're mostly used to writing introductions addressed to potential employers, you may come off as stilted and weird if you do that here. Instead, remember that this is a casual situation, you need to make your intro conversational. It can also be about things that aren't very important (like in the above example) the important thing is that you paint a positive image of yourself.

B. Dating Websites

Okay, these are basically the online versions of active locations. Here, everyone is looking for a partner, it's no secret, which means you can be straightforward about your interest in a girl. Before we go on, however, I'd like to address a very common question: Is it worthwhile to spend money on dating websites? Some sites have sign-up fees, monthly fees, whatever, should you be paying for them?

Well, it really depends on a lot of things. I think that you probably won't regret it if you do pay to be on a site, but you shouldn't force yourself if you're strapped for cash because there's lots of free sites out there that have worked just fine for other people. Always check out a dating site's reviews, especially if it requires you to pay, maybe even ask your friends about their experiences with it. Finally, it would be best if you stuck to more mainstream sites, not only are they tried and tested, but their bigger communities increase your likelihood of finding matches.

- **A Free Dating Website**

You're going to have a lot of competition here, your main goal is not just to get noticed but to get replied to. Jokes are great, but they're starting to become more common as openers, not to mention, they don't usually invite a response. You need something that grabs her attention and almost provokes a response out of her. An effective method is to give her a compliment and an assumption simultaneously.

For example, "You're one of the cutest girls here, but too bad you're a cat person. DOGS ALL THE WAY!" If her profile doesn't indicate that she owns a pet, you can say something like, "You're adorable, but it's too bad you'd rather own a horse than a dog. DOGS ALL THE WAY!" This will get her to be like, "Oh, you think you know me?" And that starts a conversation almost immediately.

A similar approach would be, "It's awesome that we have so much in common, but it's too bad you don't like spicy food, I was planning on taking you to this awesome spicy food restaurant for our first date." Note, it's always better to insult her on her *not* liking something rather than to insult her for liking something. When you insult something she likes (which is part of her identity or who she is) you're just being a douche. Instead, you should seem as if you're encouraging her to try new things that she might eventually grow to like, always bear that in mind.

Advantages	**Disadvantages**
She'll like the compliment. You'll get her to start talking, even if it seems like a bad note to start on. You can	There's a very fine line here. Make sure your insult is strong enough to get her defensive but not strong enough to

eventually calm her down as the conversation progresses and focus on common interests.	deeply offend her and get yourself blocked. Safe topics to insult her about: Preferences in animals and food. Off limits: Physical appearance, preferences in clothes and music, politics, and religion.

By the way, another reason you need to tread lightly with this opener is that it's a slippery slope. Once you get too defensive or she becomes deeply offended, it's game over, you've made an enemy. Always choose things that are relatively insignificant to your identity and hers. You can tease her by putting up a bit of a fight, but eventually you'll have to give her plenty of time to present her side and then acquiesce accordingly.

This next one works surprisingly well even though no one knows why: Send her just one word or a phrase that isn't normally used as a greeting. Some examples are: "GASP!" "Whoa." "Omelette du Fromage" (If you've been floating around 9GAG, Reddit, and/or 4chan, you'll know that this is a meme of sorts) "Yes." (Note, it's with a full stop, not "Yes?" with a question mark), even items work like, “Stapler.” “Book.” Or other things you might have lying around your desk.

Advantages	Disadvantages
It gets her attention and she’ll be thinking, “What?!” Eventually, she’ll ask you what you mean. Then you can either make up something related to the word you sent or you could be honest and say, “I just wanted to get you to reply. :)” By not using a question mark, you’re making a statement, but because it’s just a word long, it’s unconventional and will grab her attention instantly.	It breaks all dating site protocol, it doesn’t invite a response and there’s no flirt, but at least it gets the job done, somehow. Off limit words would be: body parts, anything sexual, animal sounds, basically things that have connotations.

- **A Paid Dating Website**

Paid dating communities are considerably smaller than free ones, so you don’t have to take extreme measures in order to get her attention or to have her reply to you. You could start off with, “Wow. You’re awesome.” And then, even before she replies, you can say *why* you think she’s perfect, in addition to being gorgeous, maybe she likes the same shows as you, or has similar hobbies, whatever, there must have been some reason the website matched the two of you up, focus on that common ground.

Advantages	Disadvantages
That's a pretty great compliment to start off with, she'll like it.	This isn't exactly a very memorable opener, but it gets the job done.

Another one that works well is the "I'm going to report you…" + a compliment. For example, "Okay, this isn't easy for me, but I'd feel bad if I didn't give you a heads up: I'm going to report you for stealing my heart. Any last words?" or "Just letting you know that I'm reporting you for having illegal levels of beauty."

Advantages	Disadvantages
It's playful and goofy, you can even throw in an emoticon for added goofiness.	I can't think of any at the moment, this is a fairly safe line to use.

III. Conclusion: Online

Again, this has to be my least favorite way you could meet a girl. You need to get yourself out there in real life. Most of your success depends on the quality of your profile, keep it updated, fun, and classy. Even though it's the internet, stay respectful and polite, it actually *is* possible to gain a bad reputation in an online community, may that never happen to you.

It's true that online dating has revolutionized how we meet people, but it shouldn't be your primary method of meeting people because face-to-face communication helps gives you skills and experience no amount of online dating ever could. Of course, despite my saying all of that, online dating does have promise. It's economical, easy, and exposes you to all kinds of people. Maybe someday I'll write an entire book dedicated to it, (ahem) already working (ahem) on it.

New Possibilities and Whatnot and Whatever

Obviously, there are innumerous ways to approach women, all I've done is simply highlight some of the best of them (as well as why they work and what you need to look out for). You aren't limited to these openers, their only purpose is to give you somewhere to start. I'm sure they'll serve as inspiration for the crafting of your own openers. A good exercise would be to pick an opener, then revisit Chapter 2 to see how you would apply the principles from it to the opener you picked.

With what you learned in Chapters 1-3 combined, you now have a better mindset, you now know what to say during your approach and how to say it all, but what about after the approach? It would sure be a shame if all your hard work went to waste just because you couldn't hold a conversation. Chapter

4 will help you make the best of your approach. After all, what's the point of talking to a girl if it's not going to go anywhere?

Chapter 4. Conversational Maintenance & Un-approach-ization

Plot twist: Approaching the girl was actually the easiest part, it's keeping the conversation going that's the real thing you should've been worried about and bought a how-to book for. Don't panic, it's not as bad as it sounds. Besides, after making it this far in life, I'm assuming you had to have a conversation or two. On the other hand, you might be one of those guys who thinks that he doesn't need any help with his conversation skills at all. If so, congratulations, confidence is roughly 50% of the work.

It would be helpful to remember that she'll forget most of what you say within anywhere from four seconds to a few hours, but what she will remember is the way you treated her and your overall attitude. We talked about improving your attitude and your projection of yourself in Chapter 2 but that was just the tip of the iceberg. Chapters 2 and 3 focused on helping you start a conversation on the right foot, but this chapter is going to show you how to keep dancing.

As with all the other chapters, there are lots of examples that demonstrate the principles I mention. I'm a big believer in teaching by example because examples allow you to see (or since this is a book, to imagine) how whatever it is I teach you plays out. However, don't limit yourselves to just the examples, they're just there to help you understand the points I'm trying to make, and once you understand the principle, you won't even need my example.

I think it's worth telling you in advance that almost none of the information in this chapter will be helpful to you in terms of an online conversation. This chapter is really more on honing your real life social skills as well as spontaneity. Besides, carrying on a conversation online is relatively straightforward, you don't have to worry about body language, social norms, and even timing.

Keep the Flames Alive: Beginner Mistakes to Avoid vs. Pro. Footsteps to Follow

Similar to what we did in Chapter 1, I'm first going to debunk some myths that lead to fatal mistakes. And then later I'll give you the pointers you'll need for an interesting and productive conversation. The best part is that the conversational skills you pick up when meeting people will serve you well at work and even within your family. As you go through this section, examine yourself honestly and actively search for areas that could be improved. Remember, the more honest you are with yourself, the faster you'll improve.

Common Mistakes: Asking Too Many Questions

It's true that asking questions to keep her talking is an effective way to make sure the conversation continues, but did you know that by asking too many questions you end up boring her? Yes, girls do love guys who are "great listeners" but too much of anything is bad. Why do you think girls love spending time with each other so much when almost all of them are so talkative?

It's because the other girls bring things to the conversation. Picture a conversation as a bonfire, it needs both wood and oxygen to keep it going. However, what would happen if you just sat there fanning the fire without putting in new logs? It's not wrong to give the fire more oxygen, but because you didn't put new logs in, there's nothing for the fire to consume and all the effort you spent fanning it would be completely wasted.

Similarly, there's nothing wrong with asking questions, but using *only* questions without contributing anything means there's almost nothing for you to ask about. Eventually, the conversation will just fizzle out and die. It's not a crime to talk about yourself, after all, a conversation is all about *two* people *talking*. We'll discuss this in greater detail later.

Common Mistakes: Filler Words

Some examples of filler words are: "um", "uh", "like", and "you know". Now, I'm not saying that you can never use them, but filler words are usually brought into a sentence because of one or both of the following reasons:

A. *Nervousness:* You're not used to speaking to a woman (or even to people in general) so your mind is panicking and it becomes hard to continue the thought of your sentence.

B. *Fear of Silence:* You don't want the conversation to have a pause in it for fear that it might lead to the end of the conversation, so you stall and make sounds because you think that bad conversation is better than no conversation, right?

As we established before, it's okay for the conversation to go quiet for some time, it is a perfectly normal phenomenon. In fact, silence is better than awkward filler words or phrases. Now, no one's able to avoid filler words completely and at all times, but an overuse of them is almost deafening and borderline irritating. See:

Acceptable use of filler words:	Unacceptable use of filler words:
My friends and I checked out the new pancake house that opened a few blocks from here, **you know**, the **um**, the PNCK HS. Have you tried it yet?	So **like**, **um**, my friends and I **uh**, checked out the new, **you know**, pancake house that **uh**, it **uh**, opened a few blocks from here, the **uh**, PNCK HS.

	Have you, **you know**, been there?

At first, it might seem like I'm exaggerating, surely no one talks like the example in the right column, right? WRONG. In fact, without realizing it, you might be one of those people. Pay attention to the way you speak and how you act when you're nervous. Some people tend to draw out their fillers, for example, "ummmmm..." whereas others tend to repeat them, "um, um, um," Your goal is to be part of neither of those groups.

Common Mistakes: Being Afraid of Conflict

This beginner mistake also stems from the fear of the conversation ending without any results. Some guys believe that if they just go with whatever the girl says, she'll think, "He's perfect because he likes and dislikes the exact same things as me. And if I end up going out with him, we'll never ever fight and live happily ever after." However, you don't have to become a carbon copy of her in order to get her.

It's good to show appreciation and respect for her interests and opinions, but she is also capable of showing appreciation and respect for yours. No two people are exactly the same, she knows that and is actually *expecting* conflict. Conflict is also a good way to gauge her maturity and is a glimpse into how the two of you would handle disagreements if you ever got into a serious relationship.

All in all, conflict is your friend, and since it's your friend, you need to embrace it and treat it properly. When you find something that the two of you have different opinions, first understand why she thinks what she thinks. Let her know you see where she's coming from, and then you can tactfully explain your side. You don't have to determine who's right or wrong, instead, you can just agree that everyone sees the world differently, but by keeping a cool head and showing maturity when talking to her will definitely make a memorable impression on her.

Pro. Footsteps to Follow: Practicing Answers

After learning what *not* to do, you're now in a good position to contrast all of that with what you *should* be doing. First up, you need to prepare yourself. Indeed, a soldier never marches into battle unarmed. There's nothing wrong with practicing a few answers to some common questions beforehand. In fact, doing so will actually help chop off a lot of your nervousness and will save your poor beginner brain from a ton of stress and improvisation.

Throughout this book, I've told you again and again that it all depends on your projection of yourself. You don't want to sell yourself short, instead, you want to show her that you're an awesome person and that she won't regret investing in you. As a beginner, the most efficient way to do that is by practicing answers to questions that are most likely to come up during the conversation, such as:

- What do you do for a living?
- What are your hobbies?
- What do you study/what did you study?
- What are your passions?

Make your answers interesting and natural, embellish a little. No, don't lie, and I don't want you to exaggerate, I'm just telling you to choose words that do you justice. As you gain more experience, you'll find that you'll be able to prepare less and be more spontaneous. Well, what if you there's seemingly nothing exotic about your job or your life? It's a lie, there are upsides to every job and everyone's lifestyle. However, if you seriously can't come up with anything, you can joke about the boringness of it all.

For example, she asks, "What do you do for a living?" and you work as an clerk, you can say, "Well, I'm a clerk at [Company's name]. Let me know if you ever drop by our office, I'll let you staple some reports, [sarcastically]: yay..." after joking about the boringness, you can laugh it off and say something like, "It may be boring, but I actually kind of like it," or something along those lines.

But what if your job is boring and/or you don't enjoy it? For example, let's say again that you're a clerk but it isn't exactly your dream job, then you should focus on your hobbies and dreams. For example, she asks, "What do you do for a living?" then you say, "Right now, I work as a clerk down at [Company's name], but I'm actually more of an outdoorsy person, I love hiking and running. Maybe someday I'll send you pictures of me climbing Mt. Everest..." and then laugh it off.

[DISCLAIMER: To the readers who actually work as clerks, the author is not insulting your profession. The author has previously expressed to us his appreciation for all the hard work all of you do. The author just needed to make a point and chose your profession at random and he thanks you clerks for being so understanding. The author's opinions and views do not, in any way, reflect the opinions and views of our publishing house and/or the individuals within it.]

See how easy it is to highlight the good stuff? Make it clear that regardless of what your job is now, you're someone with big dreams and things to accomplish in life. I think that at this point you especially appreciate all those things I said about making big changes in your life and living your life purposively. You could even be someone who's already at their dream job. If so, that's perfect. Let her know that you worked hard to get to where you are now, that you're a guy who has goals and actually meets them.

In conclusion, think your answers through and write them down. Practice them in front of a mirror while making eye contact with your reflection, it will help you decide whether or not to smile at certain points and whatnot. Do *not* bring your written answers with you on a night out, you can't be seen reading seemingly simple answers off of scrap papers just before you talk to someone. Instead, if you really must have them with you at all times, save the answers in notes on your phone, it'll make referring to them a lot less conspicuous.

Pro. Footsteps to Follow: Responding Properly

We've already established that asking too many questions is a big no-no, but what are you supposed to do then? You started the conversation, you can steer it where you want, and there are four main ways you can do this: asking, relating, flirting, and banter. We're going to go through them individually and see how they affect a conversation.

A. *Asking*

So you've just used your opener, both of you have introduced yourselves, now what? You can ask her how her day has been, or if she's looking forward to anything this week. Basically, you're finding out things about her. Asking questions will help make sure a conversation isn't one-sided. This is how you can best show your interest in her and she'll definitely respond to that positively.

Of course, you are already also well aware of the dangers of doing too much of this and that you should make it a point to ask open-ended questions for the best results, so we're not going to go into all of that again. As you'll see later, questions are actually really useful in resuscitating dying conversations, but we're not going into that right now, instead, let's see the next response for what you can do after she's answered your question...

B. Relating

This response allows her to find out more about you. For example, maybe she says that she plans on seeing a movie with her friends. If it's a franchise that you like or if you particularly like one or two of the actors, you can let her know. Relating helps her understand who you are and how you feel about yourself. Don't be too guarded when it comes to information about yourself because if you are, then you're either doing something illegal and don't want anyone to find out, or you have some unresolved issues with yourself.

Either way, you instantly become less attractive. You start to look more unstable and you'll make her uncomfortable. Sure, you can try being mysterious, but it's definitely best if you do so in a playful way. For example, if she asks you about your interests, then you can say, "Guess... What do I look like my hobbies would be?" it's a fun kind of light and fun mystery. A terrible way of going about it would be saying something like, "I don't want to talk about it." Or by abruptly changing the subject, that's not mysterious, it's just awkward and weird.

She might say something like, "I'm a huge fan of The Big Bang Theory." If you like it too, then say so, and don't be afraid to add emotion. For example, "Seriously? I love TBBT too!" Note that I used a strong word: "**love**" when talking about the show. Try using vivid words like that more often. Instead of, "I like..." try, "appreciate", "relish", or "enjoy". Words like that make you sound more deliberate and passionate about things in your life and it'll impress her, at least subconsciously.

Now, what if you're not into The Big Bang Theory? Let's say, you're more of a Community (created by Dan Harmon) fan. Be honest and say something like, "Oh yeah, The Big Bang Theory, I've seen a few episodes, but my all-time favorite show has got to be Community." You didn't disregard her opinion or say that your show was better, you were just relating what you like.

If she doesn't say anything after you say that, then you can ask her if she's seen a few episodes and/or tell her what it's about. You should never worry that relating something will lead to a dead end in the conversation. After relating, you can always ask her about her opinion or explain more about yours. There is no such thing as having nothing to talk about.

I mean, in this day and age, with 7 billion people in the world, literally millions of species of plants and animals, thousands of various activities mankind can carry out, advancing technology, virtually unlimited access to information, crises, breakthroughs, our planet spinning and going round and round a gigantic radioactive ball of gas surrounded by planets and other balls of gas, most of which are hundreds of times larger than our own planet in a universe so large we can't even comprehend how-

Basically, my point is that there is an endless supply of things to talk about and I think it's stupid that anyone could honestly believe there's *"nothing to talk about"*. [Drops mic] Peace out, I'm done. Just kidding, I can't leave yet, I still have so much to teach you. Moving on...

C. *Flirting*

This is what keeps you out of the dreaded friend zone. The thing is, asking and relating stuff are just basic components of conversations everywhere. You ask and relate stuff to family members, friends, and even bosses. However, flirting is what makes your conversation with a girl different from all those other conversations. I'm not exactly sure how I'm supposed to explain this because I feel like it's just like trying to explain what water tastes like.

Flirting is basically just letting her know you're interested in her romantically. Although, it works best when you pepper it throughout the conversation. Constant flirting makes you look too easy to get. The simplest way to flirt is to take whatever she says and turn it into a compliment. For example, if you guys end up having a conversation about traveling, and she happens to mention that she went to a scenic country like Hawaii then you can say, “I bet you were the most beautiful sight there.”

Of course, you want your compliments to be more than just about looks, pay attention to the little things. Maybe she has a cute laugh or is very articulate or has is smart despite not wanting to show off, whatever it is, let her know that you that you find her attractive. There’s more to flirting than just compliments, your body language should also show that you’re interested in her.

Your eyes do a lot of talking. I’d say that eye contact is 30% of the flirting. An effective way to get her heart racing would be to gaze (NOT stare, gaze) at her when she isn’t looking at you, maybe while she’s talking to one of her friends or looking around the party, and then when she notices you looking at her, you immediately look away. It’s as if you didn’t mean for her to see you looking at her, but it immediately gets her thinking, “Wait, was he looking at me? He likes me, doesn’t he? Should I bring it up?” she’s flustered because it was unexpected.

Another similar technique starts off the same way, you gaze at her while she’s busy, but this time, when she notices you looking at her, you could maintain eye contact and do the lopsided smile/smirk we talked about in Chapter 2. Again, she wasn’t expecting you to be looking at her like that, so it instantly catches her off guard. Not to mention, your calmness while she’s momentarily tripping over herself will instantly make you look way cooler than usual.

D. Banter

Initially, I wasn't sure whether to give "Banter" its own section or to make it a part of "Flirting" but I decided to give it its own section because while banter is a great way to flirt, not all banter is flirting. I guess a good way to define banter is just "messing around" and cracking jokes, and it is absolutely essential to keeping things positive and fun. Obviously, you can't banter all the time, otherwise you will look immature and she won't want to have anything to do with you.

Always smile during banter in order to let her know that you're playing. A simple form of banter is what I call "mini game shows" which are actually fun ways to answer questions. For example, if she asks you, "So, where are you from?" You can say something like, "You're a smart girl, see if you can figure it out." It keeps her on her toes and gets her to invest in the conversation.

Banter also involves absurdity. For example, if she asks you, "Where do you work?" You can say, "Oh, I'm a shoemaker, I make shoes do things. For example, if you lend me your shoes, I can make them disappear." See what I mean? The lines are completely unbelievable. However, when carrying out this kind of banter, she'll probably play along with the absurdity, which means that you have to commit to the absurdity too.

Let's say you bantered that you were best friends with Bill Nye (The Science Guy!) and she laughs but then says, "Oh yeah? Well, what's he like?" She's playing along by asking you a question. In turn, you commit by saying, "Oh, he's great! His first name is Bill and last name is Nye. He's commonly called 'The Science Guy' and uh, he's the guy who likes science and science-y things..." You answered absurdity with absurdity, it'll keep her laughing.

Finally, there's something that I can only describe as "fake meanness", this is when you're sarcastic (almost snide even) to her in a playful way. The key to showing her that you're being playful is to remark with your syllables drawn out, speaking slowly, and with a smile. Let's say that you're a pretty buff guy and she asks, "So, do you work out?" (A surprisingly common question, am I right, buff guys?) Instead of answering it right away, you can say, "Me? Nooo... Of course not... I just woke up like this one day, the universe is always nice to me like that."

Again, you want to watch the tone of your voice and to make sure that you're smiling. A nice touch would be to roll your eyes and shake your head while you say it, remember that your goal is to make her laugh. If you don't say it comically enough, you'll make her feel bad for real, so try to look like you're having fun. Finally, don't run with the banter if you sense it's getting tired. For example, the Bill-Nye-Science-Guy joke is pretty decent banter material, but if you keep bringing it back or if you talk about it for too long, then it's going to get boring and awkward.

So those are the basics of the four kinds of responses/contributions you can make to the conversation. Do your best to use all four in order to balance your conversation out. However, what you say is just as important as *how* you say it. that's the best that I can explain all of that, so I guess the only thing left to do now is to move on to the next thing you should be doing...

Pro. Footsteps to Follow: Listening

Did you know that there's even a proper way to listen? That might surprise you since listening is a passive activity, right? WRONG. Hearing is a passive activity, but listening is active. Confused? Well, "Hearing" refers to your ears taking in sounds, but "Listening" is much more than that, it refers to you actively understanding and processing the sounds (a.k.a. words) that enter your ears.

Listening properly is a way of showing the other person respect, and if you listen to them, s/he will be more likely to listen to you. I was initially surprised at how much information and research is out there on the topic of listening. People have even come up with mental exercises that are supposed to make you a better listener.

And then I realized, "Of course people have invested so much in studying it!" A conversation without anyone listening is just speaking into the air. Listening is just as part of our lives as conversation is. I may not have always consciously appreciated the beauty of listening, but that didn't make it any less important or necessary in my life. And just like there are different types of responses, there are also different forms of listening, officially, there are four:

A. *Emphatic Listening:* Its main purpose is to provide understanding and support.
B. *Informational Listening:* Carried out to gather information.
C. *Critical Listening:* Used to evaluate messages.
D. *Appreciative Listening:* Done in order to enjoy the situation (Like when you're listening to music or audiobooks).

NOTE: You probably won't need letters C. & D. in this context, but I included them because it's just nice to know these things, you know?

Also, on average, a person retains only around 25% of what s/he listens to, yikes. With this in mind, you need to make sure you make every moment count. After all, you never know what she's going to end up remembering or forgetting. Also related to our inability to remember certain things is the fact that our brains have a limited speed at which they can convert stimuli into memories, in other words, sometimes it's impossible for us to remember something because our brains never registered it in the first place (By the way, this process is called 'memory encoding', whenever you're bored, try looking it up. It's a fascinating process and a surprisingly controversial topic amongst scientists and psychologists).

You can also take advantage of the fact that our brains can process up to 500 words a minute even though human beings can only speak up to 300 words a minute. This means that there's a lot of excess brain power that isn't being utilized. You can use that excess brain power to think about questions you could ask her about what she's saying or to remember anything relevant. Sure, it takes more effort to actually pay attention and push your brain to understand what she's saying, but it's not going to kill you.

On the other hand, you shouldn't get too frustrated if you don't understand everything. If it's seemingly unimportant, then let it go. However, if you think it's a major part of what you and her are talking about, don't be afraid to ask her to rephrase it or repeat it to you. She won't think you're dumb for asking, on the contrary, she'll appreciate your attentiveness and genuine interest in what she's saying.

Pro. Footsteps to Follow: Fallback Topics

I know that we've already established that there is *always* something to talk about, but what if you're in the middle of a conversation and you feel that the conversation is starting to run dry even though neither of you have to leave just yet? What if you honestly just can't think of a new topic or simply don't know how to transition into it? You'll need to have some fallback topics stored in a drawer somewhere in your brain for use at times like these.

In short, the fallback topics are: holidays/vacations, food, stuff either you or her has mentioned before, and pets. The main advantage of having fallback topics ready is that they add to your preparedness, you'll feel less nervous because you'll be thinking, "It's okay. I'm not that nervous because no matter what happens, I have these topics I can fall back on to save myself."

Further, almost all of these fallback topics don't work so well in passive locations. Also, I personally don't think that you should extend the conversation for too long in a passive setting because she would most likely need to leave quickly and extending the conversation will just put you on her bad side. These fallbacks are more for when you're chilling with her and you both have time to kill, but the only thing dying is the conversation.

I mean, you could also just simply end the conversation by getting her contact details and walking away, then continue it online once you're more prepared instead of extending the conversation. Besides, there's no minimum time goal a conversation must last for in order for you to make a good impression. However, if you seriously want to continue the conversation some more, then that's cool too, let's go through the fallback topics and some ways you can transition into them.

First off, holidays and vacations. This is great because you're bringing back good memories and it'll get the two of you feeling positive and nostalgic, so it should improve the overall atmosphere of the conversation and get it flowing. None of these fallback topics require any setup, you can just insert them whenever things get quiet or if you've used up the energy of the conversation and can't think of anything to say because you barely know her. For example, once you've reached the end of a topic and things are silent, wait for a second and then say, "I don't know why, but I just remembered my trip to…" and carry on from there.

You can also begin with, "You know, I was thinking of traveling somewhere warm to escape from this fridge of a city, any recommendations?" Of course, if you live in a place that's warm and sunny all the time, then you can change the line into something about trying to escape the heat. You can insert this line before things go completely silent, "This is nice, the last time I felt this [relaxed/good] was when I was on vacation in…" And finally, if you're talking to her during a weekend night out, you can say, "Ah, I can't believe that it's back to work again Monday. Do you have any idea when the next [holiday/break] is? I could seriously use a break."

The next thing you can talk about is food. Similar approach, when you feel the conversation start to slow down, let it go silent for a second or two and then bring the topic of food up with, "Wow, for some reason I'm starving all of a sudden, what about you?" or "Just curious, do they serve _____ here? I think I'm suddenly starting to crave some." If her only response is, "No, I don't think they serve them here, [giggle]" and then she goes silent again, you can fake frustration and go, "Man, that's too bad. I'd really like some ____ right about now. Do you know what that feels like?" or "Have you ever felt that way about _____?"

It's always best to start off with yourself when it comes to food because some girls are oversensitive and may think that you're implying they're fat if you start off focusing on them and food. By talking about yourself first and then casually asking her if she feels the same way, you're silently signaling to her subconscious, "Look, I'm hungry and I'm asking if you're hungry too, but I'm not accusing you of being extraordinarily hungry as if you have an eating disorder." So she'll be more likely to respond in a positive way.

Next, you could always refer back to something that she said at an earlier point in the conversation. Of course, use discretion. I'm not saying that it's okay to repeat everything that you said word for word, but you could take the previous topic and give it a bit of a spin. For example, let's say that she mentioned that she works at a boutique and you guys already talked about the name of the store and its location, but you can recall that topic and say, "This might sound random, but I remembered what you said about working at [Store Name] downtown? I was just wondering, did they give you a special [test/some training] on things like customer service or how to recommend stuff you think the customer would like?"

See? It's the same topic, just remixed and with a different aspect highlighted. And just in case some of you are still wondering, yes, you can do it with any topic because it's a simple step-by-step process. First, pick a topic the two of you talked about earlier, it can be simple or complicated, something you mentioned, something that she mentioned, it makes no difference. Next, ask yourself, "What have we already covered under this topic? What makes this topic interesting? How does this topic affect her personally? How does it affect me personally?" Then you'll start to see all kinds of aspects of the topic that you haven't talked about yet. Easy.

Pets are like fuzzy little superheroes here to save the conversation. Dog owners, here's a good one, "By the way, can you please check what time it is?" and no matter what she mentions say, "Oh, okay. I should leave in around [two hours/thirty minutes, etc.] if I want to make it home in time to take [Dog's Name] out for [his/her] walk." Smooth as heck, eh? But if you don't own a dog, then you can still keep the same general format, but just change the last part from "...take [Dog's Name] for [his/her] walk" to "...give [Pet's Name] [his/her] food."

Of course, it would be weird if you started talking about pets and then tell her that you don't own one, it'll be too obvious that you're trying to save the conversation. Your goal is to save the conversation without her realizing that it needs saving. So choose your fallback topics and prepare your material under them well in advance. No, not a script, but at least a general outline or list of related experiences and things that you could mention, it would be best to have at least three fallbacks. Not to mention, you can even create your own fallback topics that invoke positive feelings and can be brought up at any point in the conversation.

All Good Things Must Come to An End... Temporarily

So you did it. You made some changes, settled some issues, prepared yourself, went out with your friends, walked up to a girl, did your opener, and now here you are, just the two of you having a great conversation and the time of your lives. While you're talking, you imagine your future with this beautiful girl. You think about what your first date would be like, meeting her parents, her meeting your parents, moving in together, your proposal, your wedding day, honeymoon, your first chil-

"Well, this has been fun, but my ride's here and I gotta go. Thanks for the laughs!" She suddenly says seemingly out of nowhere as she turns around and walks away from you and the beautiful future you had planned for the both of you. With every step she takes away from you, you can hear your heart scream, "Nooooo!" in slow motion and your knees buckle from underneath you as everything fades to black and-

Sounds like a nightmare, doesn't it? And okay, okay, I may have exaggerated it a teensy weensy bit, but you have to agree that it's a fact that no one likes having their hard work wasted. What if you genuinely liked the girl and she seemed to like you back but then never saw her again? Don't panic, I'm here to make sure that you *do* see her again. Yes, all conversations end eventually, what's important is that you're able to pick up where you left off.

You need to know in advance how and when you're going to end the conversation so that you can control it. It's always better that you end it rather than letting her end it. You know how they say you should quite while you're ahead? That is exactly what you should be doing. End the conversation before things go downhill and she actually looks for ways to try and "escape" the conversation.

Getting Contact Details (The Right Way)

I guess the best part about this part of the conversation is that you don't really need to transition into this. While convention dictates that this happens towards the end of the conversation, getting someone's contact information can actually happen any time between the middle of up to just before the end of the conversation. Another convention is that you have to get her *phone number*, but in this day and age, I think it's more practical to add her on Facebook or some other social media platform.

Just to clarify: I'm not a fan of using the internet to meet people (which I'm sure I made very clear in Chapter 3), but I'm certainly not blind to the advantages of using the internet to keep in touch with people you've already met. I am very much aware of and am very appreciative of mankind's advances in technology and the potential they hold to improve our lives... for crying out loud, I'm not a dinosaur.

Anyway, your goal is to get her number or a way to continue chatting with her online, or both. And just like there are lines for starting a conversation, you can be sure that there are lines for ending one.

Here are just some effective and confident ones:

- "Well, this has been so much fun, but I need to get back to my friends. Sorry about that, I really would love to stay longer but anyway, just type in your [phone number/Facebook username] here and let's talk again."

Advantages	Disadvantages
Notice that you're not asking her, "Can I have you're number?" You're telling her to give you her contact info, talk about exhuming confidence.	It sounds slightly cold and generic.

- "I really enjoyed this, and unless you want to meet here every day at the same time for the rest of our lives, I suggest you give me your [phone number/name on Facebook] and we can have this much fun more often."

Advantages	Disadvantages
Humorous and light. This is especially smooth if you insert it right after banter since this technically is banter. And again, you're not asking for her number, you're politely demanding it.	I don't think there are any, seems like a pretty safe line to me.

- You could promise to send her pictures of something. For example, you can mention that you have a pet and then say, "Give me your <u>[number/Instagram/Facebook]</u> and I'll add you and grant you access to some of the cutest photos on the internet."

Advantages	Disadvantages
You can adapt this to any of your hobbies, whether it's cooking, outdoorsy stuff, travel, etc. just remember to change the adjective from "the cutest photos on the internet" to something like, "the most epic photos..." or "the tastiest looking food..." in order to match whatever you promised to show her.	You can only use this if you've kept your profile up to date. This may sound hard to believe, but girls stalk us too. So once she accepts your request, she'll be scrutinizing your profile to see if it lives up to what you described it as.

It sounds like you're doing her a favor by adding her.	

Now, as established before, rejection is real, you're not going to be successful every single time. And sadly, even at this stage, there is the chance that you will be rejected, things could be going well in the conversation but when you ask her for her number, she suddenly makes an excuse and walks away. You need to be ready for anything, which is why the following sections will deal with rejection and success separately.

- **Success!**

So she's agreed to give you her contact details. NICELY DONE! However, you still have to watch how you behave because you don't want to leave a bad final impression. The biggest and most common rookie mistake is acting as if she's doing you such a huge favor by giving you her number. Don't let out a huge sigh of relief or thank her profusely once she gives the okay.

Can you imagine how weird that would look? Let's put ourselves in her shoes for a minute. This confident, playful, stable guy comes up to us, says a killer opener, and then has a fun conversation with us. However, once we agreed to give this guy our number/username all of a sudden he starts thanking us and acting as if no girl has ever done this before. And now we wonder, "Is something wrong with him? Why is he making such a big deal over something so simple?" and all of a sudden, we're starting to question everything we know about this guy and we start feeling as if we can't trust him.

Sobering, isn't it? So. What *should* you do instead? If she gives you her number, then ask her to type it in your cellphone herself. Also, it would be better if you could casually find out her last name while you're saving the number. For example, you get your phone back after Cathy's finished punching in her number, then you can say, "Cool, thanks. [While typing] Cathy... Cath- Oh, sorry, what did you say your last name was again?" Of course, getting her last name is somewhat optional, but it's worth a shot so that you can have a look at her Facebook or Instagram later.

Smile politely at her just to show that you're please, but you're not overjoyed. You don't have to make any more conversation, you can just say, "Alright, thanks for a fun conversation, I'll be sure to message you and we can do it again sometime." Or some kind of variation of this line. What's important is that what you say is relaxed, positive, and casual. You don't want to show too much commitment in the beginning because it would be putting pressure on her and it'll scare her away.

Another problem you could run into when you're too excited is trying to set up a date immediately. Ugh, dude, no. And I just know that some of you are thinking, "Well, why not? What's wrong with that?" Answer: EVERYTHING. You can banter about getting married or taking her to swim with the sharks because it's obvious that you're kidding. However, if you're already seriously trying to set up a meeting/date with her, it shows her that you obviously have nothing better to do in your life and that you're overexcited that you finally found someone.

Instead, play it cool and wait for a little bit. Wait until at least the following day before sending her a message, and make sure that the two of you have been talking for at least a week before you ask to meet up again. Remember, you need to be relaxed, but that's not the same thing as not caring for her. Of course you should care for and respect her, but show some respect for her personal space and maintain your dignity.

- **Rejection**

Alright, so she's decided that she'd rather not give you her details, that's fine. Remember how we talked about making sure that you didn't show that you were too happy or excited if you happen to succeed in getting her number? Well, in this case, you have to make sure that you don't show that you're too bummed out. A truly stable person doesn't get upset over things like this.

You don't have to prove yourself to anyone, so if she doesn't feel like having another conversation again, then it shouldn't affect your self-esteem. Make sure that you stay respectful, her decision to not talk doesn't make her a bad person. Further, getting rejected doesn't make you a bad person either. It's not always your fault, but think of this as an opportunity to grow and learn from your mistakes.

An appropriate response would be something like, "Oh, I see, alright then. Well, thanks for the good conversation anyway." Then simply walk away. I've seen some idiots completely flip out when they get rejected, and it only makes everything worse. Mostly because if you react like that, you draw attention to yourself and you're basically announcing to the world that you got rejected and that you're petty and childish enough to start throwing tantrums like some five-year-old.

Don't say things like, "Well, it's your loss," or, "It's fine, I didn't even like you that much anyway," or start swearing at her because honestly the only person you'll be hurting with those harsh words is yourself. She's an adult who has the right to choose who she wants and doesn't want to speak to. All in all, by being respectful, composed, and dignified, you could actually make her regret not giving you her number, and the best part of all is that you'll be showing respect for yourself.

ERROR 404: Conclusion Not Found

This chapter doesn't have much of a conclusion since the next chapter is basically one giant conclusion where I also sum up some of the main points from this chapter and the previous chapters, but I guess there's still a few more things we can say about keeping up a conversation.

I hope this chapter has shown you that although conversation is an important and complex process, it's actually not that hard to keep one going. Not only are there fallback topics, but you have been having conversations your whole life and you've been just fine without my glorious guidance and mentorship. This chapter focused on some of the elements of a conversation, but my goal wasn't to scare you, it was just to highlight some of the things that you might take for granted because paying attention to them would substantially improve the quality of your conversations.

Chapter 5. Conclusion: The End Is Nigh!

Wow. So this is it. This is where my mentorship ends. Quick question though, did you learn anything? Like, seriously. It's honestly been so much fun writing all of this out for you, but I didn't write this just so that I could have fun. I wrote this to change your perspective of yourself and the art of successfully approaching women. I did this to help the guys who didn't even dare approach women simply because they overestimated how difficult approaching them could be.

And I also sort of did it because I've always wanted to feel like a Kung-Fu-Master- Person-Thing. You know what I mean, like those wise old guys with legions of students. Well, what has this master *taught* you so far? ANSWER: A LOT. But the real question we should be answering is, "How much did you actually *learn* and apply in your life?"

I can teach you all I want, but if you're not picking any of it up, then I might as well pull a Tom Hanks and start talking to coconuts (By the way, everyone who knows which movie that reference is from automatically gets an A+ from me in living life to the full). Now, I don't like picking favorites, but in this case I have no choice, I'll have to pick a few highlights/favorites of some of my words of wisdom because, let's face it, some wisdoms are more important than others.

I've taught you lots of specific rules (there's been an insane amount of Dos and Don'ts throughout the book), but it would be so much better if you grasped the principles behind them. Some of you might be wondering, "Hang on, is there even a difference between a *rule* and a *principle*?" Well, let's answer that with an example. Let's take the rule, "Drivers shouldn't drink alcohol and drive." This rule is based on the principle, "Drivers should be focused on the road while they're driving." And I believe that the principle is superior to the rule, but why?

Continuing with our example, let's say that I don't drink and drive, *however*, I text and drive instead. I could reason, "I'm not breaking the law, there's no rule against texting and driving in this city, so I can text and drive all I want." And technically, I would be right. I'm not breaking the ***rule*** (a.k.a. "law") since I'm honestly not drinking and driving, however, I'm still in danger and am still a danger to other people because I'm compromising the ***principle*** that drivers should be focused on the road while they're driving.

Similarly, this book is chockfull of both rules and principles. Rules are more straightforward to pick up since they're so specific. For example, in Chapter 1, we learned the rule, "Never approach a woman from behind." That instruction is easy enough to understand and follow, but it's somewhat harder to find the principle behind it because principles are broader and subtler. In this case, the guiding principle is, “Don’t spring any unpleasant surprises on a woman.”

In order to simplify your search for the principles driving the rules, I’m now going to discuss some of the guiding principles for each of the chapters:

Chapter:	**Guiding Principles**
1.	The ability to approach women is neither hereditary nor inherent to anyone or anything.
	Don’t believe everything you see onscreen or read on the internet, the best way to find out more about approaching women is by getting out there and actually doing it.
	Rejection is real and inevitable, the only thing you can do is face it head on.
2.	You can’t be happy with someone or expect them to be happy with you unless you’re first happy with yourself.
	The only person you have to prove yourself to is yourself.
	Set goals that are both outside of your comfort zone and reasonable.
	Everyone has flaws, but what matters the most is that you’re working on them.
	Balance is everything. Too much of anything will never work out.
3.	Be respectful, calm, and positive because no one wants to be around a downer/douche.
	What you say is just as important as how you say it.

	You don't have to apologize for being sociable, all human beings have a right to be sociable
	All openers that are light, clear, and appropriate work well.
	Openers that are crude, needy, or thoughtless will never work.
4.	Holding a conversation is actually trickier than starting one, but you'll get better with practice.
	A little preparation goes a long way. Further, preparing ahead of time is the most natural course for a beginner.
	Stay away from topics like politics, religion, etc. because those are too personal. You can talk about that stuff after you guys become good friends, but they are highly inappropriate topics for a first time conversation.
	There is always, ALWAYS something to talk about.

There you go, just some of the bare bones that the entire book is based on. Highlight and mark stuff that you especially want to remember or try out. Set aside time each week to either go out with your friends to meet new people or work through your personal Issues. I'm no psychiatrist, so I'm not exactly an expert in working through issues and whatnot, but I've been there.

No one's perfect, which means that everyone's struggling with one thing or another, Just make sure to fight your battles and *win*. However, that you don't become so obsessed with improving yourself to be better company for other people that you forget to actually be with other people. Again, balance, balance, balance. And balance. I know it would've sounded better if I just said "balance" three times, but three's an odd number, so I added a fourth "balance" to balance it all out. Ha. Weird, I know. Am I insane? Nope, just a genius. Anyway, back to the matter at hand...

You *will* get turned down and you *will* feel terrible for it, but when that happens, I want you to remember that the only time you're a loser is when you start labeling yourself as one. People can say or do whatever they want to you, but it's up to you to decide whether you're going to let any of that bother you. My advice: Don't let it bother you. At the end of the day, it's your life, we write our stories, and you shouldn't let them narrate or decide what happens.

However, you need to maintain an open mind towards learning. After you're done with the last page of this book, go see what other dating gurus have to say- By the way, just to clarify, I am *not* a dating guru. Please don't call me a dating guru, I'm not much of a fan of the way it sounds, "guru". I mean, just listen to it, "goo-roo", UNACCEPTABLE. I'm too great to be called a "goo-roo", why? Because what I do isn't something mystical or whatever like some guru, what I do is art. Therefore, I'm a dating *maestro*.

Anyway, as I was saying before I so rudely interrupted myself, this book is a good start, but I don't recommend limiting yourself to a single maestro. Maybe you have friends who happen to be very adept at approaching women, you can and should ask them for advice. Maybe you've heard of certain men who teach at "academies" which teach nothing but the art of approaching women, see what their advice is too. You'll be able to learn from more people's mistakes and experiences without having to learn the exact same lessons the hard way.

Of course, use your head. Don't just believe everything you hear and always weigh your options. Analyze whatever it is you learn and try to determine whether or not it would suit a specific situation. As you practice and gain more experience, all of this will become second nature to you and, who knows? You might even end up publishing your own book on how to approach women (By the way, if you ever do, I demand a 20% royalty. After all, I did make a contribution to getting you on track, 20% would be a nice way to say thank yo- Just kidding, just kidding. You don't owe me anything... I guess).

One last thing, please don't use the things you learn from me or from any other dating gurus to hurt any woman. I wrote this book to help you find someone you could be happy with because, yes, the feeling of having someone there for you is indescribably awesome. It's true that no one needs a significant other just to be happy, but good times get so much better when you share them with other people. I genuinely hope you guys each find someone, I'll be rooting for all of you.

I know that the whole theme of this book has been to keep things light and casual, but always remember that the girls you will be dealing with are real people with feelings of their own. Those feelings are things you should never take lightly or treat casually. All in all, I'm sure that you finally understand my epic introduction at the very beginning of the book and I can only hope that you have also grasped the significance of this conclusion.

It's been great being your mentor and all, but if I don't end this book, then you'll never get the chance to get out there and practice. So... yeah. Bye for real this time. And by the way, my apologies that I couldn't answer every single one of your questions, book writing isn't exactly very conducive to two-way communication and conversati- Oh, sorry, I was supposed to be ending it. Right. I'm seriously gonna stop talking now. Bye!

END